HAPPINESS ONLY IN THE NEXT

HAPPINESS ONLY IN THE NEXT

◆

SEVEN CHOICES FOR ETERNAL LIFE

David Paul Eich

iUniverse, Inc.
New York Lincoln Shanghai

HAPPINESS ONLY IN THE NEXT

SEVEN CHOICES FOR ETERNAL LIFE

Copyright © 2006 by David Paul Eich

All rights reserved. No part of this book may be used or reproduced by any means, graphic, electronic, or mechanical, including photocopying, recording, taping or by any information storage retrieval system without the written permission of the publisher except in the case of brief quotations embodied in critical articles and reviews.

iUniverse books may be ordered through booksellers or by contacting:

iUniverse
2021 Pine Lake Road, Suite 100
Lincoln, NE 68512
www.iuniverse.com
1-800-Authors (1-800-288-4677)

ISBN-13: 978-0-595-39273-5 (pbk)
ISBN-13: 978-0-595-67683-5 (cloth)
ISBN-13: 978-0-595-83669-7 (ebk)
ISBN-10: 0-595-39273-3 (pbk)
ISBN-10: 0-595-67683-9 (cloth)
ISBN-10: 0-595-83669-0 (ebk)

Printed in the United States of America

Contents

PROLOGUE 1
THE PURSUIT OF HAPPINESS 5
CHOICE #1 WEALTH or POVERTY 28
CHOICE #2 SELF or OTHERS 36
CHOICE #3 QUALITY or QUANTITY 46
CHOICE #4 FIDELITY or BETRAYAL 55
CHOICE #5 CONVICTION or COMPLACENCY 63
CHOICE #6 PRIDE or PROPER PRIDE 77
CHOICE #7 FORGIVENESS or CONDEMNATION 88
THE CALLING 98
EPILOGUE 107
NOTES 113
KEYNOTE PRESENTATIONS AND RETREATS 115

ACKNOWLEDGMENTS

I would like to acknowledge a number of people who made this work possible. Beginning with my editor Robert Polk whose patience, gentle criticism, and thought provoking commentary are reasons why every writer needs a teacher. I had the best.

Jill Oesterle is with out a doubt, the finest executive assistant I have ever had the honor of working with. Her attention to detail and mastery of the computer made my job a lot easier. Thank you, Jill.

To my Cindy whose love of her family includes a husband who disappeared on countless evenings to finish a simple little paragraph, or not-so-simple chapter, that necessitated time away from his best friend. I love you Honey.

A father would have nothing to say of importance were it not for his children. To Robbie, Andrew, and Kelly, I am truly blessed for the child-hood memories that make me proud to have earned the right to be your dad.

A special acknowledgement goes out to all who trusted me to tell their story. From friends and family to colleagues and strangers, I have been touched by you and now have the accountability to touch others. I will do my best to share your journey.

To the Blessed Mother, whose words to Saint Bernadette jump-started both my heart and computer to capture what I hope will be the reader's catalyst to eternal happiness. I am forever grateful.

And finally to my first grandchild, Natalie Rose, who has already given Granddad and Nana a reason to treasure the happiness God gives us in this life. It is to her I dedicate this book.

PROLOGUE

In 1943 Twentieth Century Fox released a new film based on the writings of Franz Werfel entitled *The Song of Bernadette,* starring newcomer Jennifer Jones. This true story of peasant girl Bernadette Soubirous and her miraculous encounter with a vision of a beautiful lady is responsible for millions of visitors who, over the past 146 years, have traveled to Lourdes, France to experience one of the most revered religious shrines in the world. More important, the story of Bernadette is about a promise that there is something more to look forward to in the world to come. This covenant was best illustrated when the lady said to Bernadette, "I cannot promise you happiness in this world, only in the next."

I have seen the film at least a dozen times, but for some unexplained reason my latest viewing triggered a puzzling reaction to that single line. The words stayed with me for days. Did the lady mean that we will never experience happiness in this world? Was she suggesting that we shouldn't waste our time searching for something that only Heaven can provide? And what about our right to pursue happiness? Surely God would not object if we explored what life has to offer.

I decided that the "pursuit of happiness," as mentioned in the Declaration of Independence, is a good thing. I also decided to search the Internet to see if there is a formula, process, or roadmap one can follow that will provide the necessary insurance needed to obtain happiness. Astonishingly, I learned that there were 2.5 million references on the topic.

This discovery led to a few simple questions: How many different ways can one person communicate the "how to" of happiness? How does one achieve it? What do people do to keep it? After careful review of the first 200 sources I learned that the quest for this evasive goal has multiple options. Website after website enticed this browser with such invitations as, "The art of…" "The way to…" and "The process for…"

Advertisers offer camps, clubs, tips, tests, agencies, resources, journals, newsletters, articles, galleries, seminars, retreats, columns, and a host of experts all willing to help me find the road to happiness.

There are special happiness groups. Parents have a unique site. Women too have their domain. Searchers from different races or cultures can differentiate which path to follow. Those interested in raising their self-esteem are invited to log-on. I can register for "authentic happiness," "profound happiness," or "full happiness." There are opportunities to sign-up for "happiness hikes," take "happiness vitamins," or even participate in "happiness hypnosis." And for those who complain that there is so little time, a site guaranteeing the "secret of happiness" in only six weeks is available. Even atheists and agnostics are encouraged to participate with articles like, "Godless happiness. What's faith got to do with it?"

Searching further I came across a *USA Today* article from December 8, 2002, announcing, "*Psychologists now know what makes people happy.*" The writer of the column opened with, "The happiest people surround themselves with family and friends, don't care about keeping up with the Joneses next door, lose themselves in daily activities and, most important, forgive easily." I didn't bother to compare the author's opinion with the other 2,494,389 Internet sources. Nor did I check out any of the more than 700 books with the word "happiness" in their title.

Readers have so many options. There is the "Happiness Instruction Kit," "Happiness in a Box," Happiness Makeover," and "Happiness on Seven Dollars a Week." You can "humm" your way to happiness, discover Karma, nature, or your path to happiness, find your "keys" to happiness, or simply learn the science and secrets of happiness. For those who are mathematically inclined, you have "Nine Pillars of Happiness," "Ten Laws of Happiness," or "Twelve Simple Secrets of Happiness." If you like a good mystery, check out "The Goddess of Happiness," the "Sonic Order of Happiness," the "Alchemy of Happiness," or the "Magic of Happiness."

After completing my cursory Internet research on the subject, I came to the conclusion that no one in this world appears to have the blueprint for this most elusive desire. Perhaps, I thought, a simple review of the dictionary or thesaurus would lead to clues as to how one could find and maintain happiness. Words and phrases like "good luck," "good fortune," "prosperity," "blessedness," "bliss," and "felicity" all did their best to describe what happiness is but failed to confirm how one achieves permanence. Even the Catholic Encyclopedia with five pages of historical, philosophical, theological, and psychological commentary failed to answer a simple question: Why did the mysterious lady say to Bernadette, "I cannot promise you happiness in this world, only in the next."

Her words motivated me to write this book as I believe too many people are desperately searching for happiness in this troubled world without weighing the opportunity to experience happiness in the next. If you believe in Heaven and wish to go there, you will find the discussions that follow helpful. If you believe in Hell and wish not to go there, then what you hold in your hands may be of greater value. If, however, you believe that there is nothing beyond this world and the "pursuit of happiness" is life's only goal, then I cordially invite you to put the book aside. After all, there are tens of thousands of websites at your disposal. Ultimately, though, there will come a time in your life when you will ponder, "Is that all there is?"

When that day comes I trust you will remember where you laid this little book. If you do take the time to read it, I believe two things will occur. First, you will reach the same conclusion I did: That what you do with your life and all it has to offer *will* determine if "eternal happiness" is waiting in the next. And second, you will take the necessary steps needed to achieve what the Mother of God promised Bernadette almost 150 years ago.

THE PURSUIT OF HAPPINESS

A LOOK BACK

On December 8, 1947, I arrived in Black River Falls, Wisconsin, courtesy of my mom and dad, Julie and Harry Eich. Six months later my Scottish-born mother divorced my father and took her son to Michigan. She made two other key decisions: never to remarry and never to return to her family in Scotland. In those days most children had two parents living at home, grandparents to visit, and brothers or sisters to play with. Though I had none of these, I can honestly say that my childhood was *not* an unhappy affair. I guess it's difficult to miss what you never had.

As far back as I can remember, my mom always worked hard to put food on the table and a roof over our heads. To me our 600-square-foot house was all we needed. She was home most evenings and weekends, and when that wasn't possible, there were always neighbors who agreed to watch over the little boy who had no father, brothers, sisters, aunts, uncles, or grandparents. My family was my mom and that was all that mattered.

In 1952, after a day at the beach, I suddenly came down with a viral infection. That evening I became so ill that my mother called a doctor who agreed to come to the house. Five days later my mother's worst fears were confirmed: Her son had polio. Three months would pass before I would return home crippled and very weak. The doctors informed my mother I would walk again but only with the help of braces. I was five years old.

But through the grace of God and my mom's special devotion to the Blessed Virgin Mary, not to mention countless hours of therapy, I learned to walk again. A few years later I was strong enough to try out for the baseball team.

To this day I remember all the boys in the neighborhood going to that first practice eagerly awaiting instructions as to who would play what position. After throwing the ball around for a few minutes, the coach yelled out, "All right, boys, I want you to run to the position you think you would most like to play." I raced out to shortstop. To my dismay the coach walked out to where I was standing and said, "David, you can't play this position because you are left-handed." It never occurred to me that catching the ball with one hand or the other had anything to do with a little boy's baseball dreams. I was directed to the first-base position, which was reserved for those of us who didn't throw with the right hand. I didn't understand this decision and there was no one at home who could explain to me why a "lefty" couldn't play shortstop.

Another "critical" decision was made that day. When it came time for me to step up to the plate, I noticed all the boys holding their bat on their right shoulder. I followed suit. Fifteen years later while playing for the base Air Force team I decided to turn to the left side and discovered that I not only could see the ball better but also had a much quicker bat. And three years ago at age fifty-five I went with my son Andrew to the batting cages where I still could "turn" on a 90-mile-an-hour fastball from the left side. Had a father, older brother, uncle, or grandparent been around that first day of my baseball "career," things might have been much different.

During my elementary and high school years, I discovered that having a Scottish mother was no advantage when it came to learning division, memorizing American history, or studying the geography of the United States. Perhaps that's why the nuns suggested that higher education would be a reach for me. Thinking back, discussions of college, trade school, the Peace Corps, or military service never took place in my home. Neither did the subject of "girls" or sex education surface at the dinner table. I was pretty much on my own to make whatever decisions I felt necessary.

On August 22, 1967, I kissed my mother good-bye and left home to join the Air Force. I knew I would soon be drafted and likely end up in Vietnam. War was not the issue. Serving my country for two years (if I lived) and coming home with little or no career training made no sense to me. Another decision was made without family counsel.

Reflecting back on my youth and teenage years, I don't ever remember having discussions with my friends about what would make us happy. Nor do I remember hearing others commenting that living with a single parent, having polio, never experiencing a male role model, or choosing four years of military experience over a four-year degree would lead to unhappiness. It was just the way it was.

I suppose daily doses of "happiness" were fed by the same experiences most young people encounter today. There were sports, school functions, friendships, jobs, and of course relationships with the opposite sex. For some unfortunate students, alcohol, drugs, pornography, and any number of antisocial behaviors offered temporary contentment. But for most of us, getting an 'A', making the team, going to the prom, having good friends, hearing the words, 'you're hired,' or 'I love you,' satisfied our short-term search for happiness.

I guess we took for granted that there was no guarantee that these experiences would last forever. High school days would end. Military or college years had a finite timetable. And that first, second, and third job would be nothing more than steps on the career ladder. Perhaps this "live-today-for-tomorrow-you-die" attitude paralleled what we intuitively knew: Time would pass; things would change; and at the end of each of our lives we would know whether or not what we did or failed to do was worth it.

Somewhere during my high school education I recall reading the Declaration of Independence. The fifty-six members of the Second Continental Congress who signed this famous document gave birth to our nation on July 4, 1776. And today, 230 years later, generations are still both empowered and perplexed by a single statement found in the beginning of the second paragraph: "*We hold these truths to be self-evident: that all men are created equal; that they are endowed by their Creator with certain inalienable Rights; that among these are Life, Liberty, and the pursuit of Happiness.*" This last phrase represents our greatest challenge.

THROUGH THE EYES OF OTHERS

Most of us have experienced happy times, events, and people. And with those experiences comes the understanding that real "happiness" is too often short-lived. Maybe that's why well-intentioned people continually resurface with a menu of ideas proposing what will or will not lead to that elusive prize. Yet the roadmap always seems to be dotted with the same signposts: money, health, career, relationships, material things, power, prestige, and praise. And though our advisors mean well, it's obvious that they themselves rarely achieve what they preach. Fortunately there is another set of consultants who seldom offer advice about what will make us happy; instead, they provide humbling examples that point us in the right direction. The following people, both young and old, have taught me invaluable lessons about the nature and source of happiness.

Brandon

As a baseball coach I had the honor of teaching and inspiring young boys to do their best while at the same time enjoy the moment. If there's one lesson parents and coaches should learn, it is this: The ground ball between the legs, the called strike three, and the game-ending dropped fly ball are long forgotten moments after the taste of ice cream.

Brandon was a little boy from Brazil who had beautiful brown eyes. While he stood on first base, his coach leaned over and said, "Brandon, on the next pitch I want you to steal." "Got it, Coach," my confident ten-year-old responded. The pitch was on its way when Brandon broke for second base. For some reason he stopped halfway to the bag. "Brandon," I yelled, "get back to the base." By now the other team's entire infield was chasing my player as he desperately ran for safety. "You're out!" yelled the umpire. The inning was over. The game was over. And I went over to one sad little boy who stood between first and second base mystified as to what he had done or failed to do. I put my hands on his little shoulders and asked, "Brandon, what happened?" Looking up at me with tears welling in his eyes he said, "Coach, I'm sorry, I guess I'm just a little boy who got confused." That day Brandon and I enjoyed a large dish of chocolate ice cream—guaranteed to remind both of us what's important in life.

Robbie

When my son Robbie was four years old, he had an accident that taught his father about life's priorities. I was standing in the kitchen feeding Robbie's younger brother, Andrew, who was busy turning his face into one giant "Spaghetti O." Their mother had chosen to leave the care of her sons in the capable hands of Dad. As Robbie ran behind the counter, he tripped on a rug and went headlong into the metal frame of the patio door. Hearing a CLUNK I quickly turned to see my son's face covered in blood. Numerous tears followed. The phrase "it looks worse than it is," conveniently applicable to head wounds, didn't reduce my anxiety as I frantically reached for a rag to clean the blood out of my son's eyes followed by a desperate call to my sister-in-law who was both a nurse and lived two blocks away.

I rushed Robbie to the hospital emergency room hoping that he would only need a few stitches and that his mother would not give me a reason to get my own. Just before the doctor began to sew the wound, my little boy reached up and said, "Daddy, please don't leave me." At that moment the pain in my heart was far greater than the pain in his head. Nothing, absolutely nothing, was more important in life. At the end of the day it was not the son who comforted his Dad, as much as it was a Dad who was comforted by his son.

Andrew

A third encounter was a not-so-gentle reminder that children often need something more than what parents think is important. My wife would religiously walk a couple of miles every morning with her neighbor friend. One day as Cindy was tying her walking shoes, five-year-old Andrew raced into the family room and proudly announced: "Mommy, I'll get my tennis shoes, and you and I can go for a walk." Cindy smiled and gently said, "Andrew, honey, you know that Mom and Mrs. Chordas walk every morning. Perhaps we can go some other time." Hoping against hope this loving mother dared to ask, "You understand, don't you, son?" Andrew, looking up at his mom said, "Yes, Mommy, I understand. Mrs. Chordas is your friend and I'm your son!" It took the entire weekend to remove the stake from my wife's heart.

The phrase, "out of the mouth of babes" has earned its reputation in many a home and on many a ball diamond. But sometimes the person who has the greatest impact on how we look at life is someone we know nothing about.

The Man with No Face

A number of years ago I was making a sales call on an automotive advertising executive. I had never met this gentleman and knew little about him or his organization. Sitting outside his office, the receptionist asked, "Have you ever met Mr. Anderson?" I explained that this was my first visit to his office. At that the lady quietly said, "Well, let me prepare you. You are about to meet a monster." Startled, I didn't know if she was referring to his management style or physical appearance. Continuing she said, "Let me explain. A few years ago Mr. Anderson and his wife were in a terrible car accident. She burned alive and he was horribly scarred for life." But she added, "Regardless, you will never meet a finer, more upbeat person."

At that moment a voice on the intercom interrupted. "Peggy, has David arrived?" "Yes, Mr. Anderson, I'll send him right in." Gesturing to his office I couldn't help but notice her comforting smile. I took a deep breath and proceeded to meet the "monster" behind the door. Mr. Anderson was standing behind his desk with his back to me. He was gazing out of his third-story window. Without turning around he said, "David, have you ever seen a bad day?" Recalling the receptionist's warning, I managed a timid response. "Well, sir, I believe we have all seen or experienced a bad day." "Come over here and I'll show you what a bad day looks like," he retorted.

Preparing for the worst I slowly walked behind his desk toward the statuesque man. Just before I reached the spot next to him, Mr. Anderson turned and smiled with a face that was no more. "David," he said, "Let me show you what a bad day looks like." With that he turned toward the window again and pointed to the ground below. Adjacent to the office complex was a cemetery! "David," he continued, "now that's a bad day. You and are I are about to have a good day." We did.

How can one who lost both his wife and face cope? How did he manage to keep a positive mental outlook? What was it like to go to the grocery store, travel on business, or attend school functions, knowing that virtually every person he encountered would either respond in shock or poorly hide their pity? Was it humanly possible to believe that this man could ever find happiness again? Ten years later I would meet another whose forbearance demanded an answer to the same question.

A Ninety-year-old Teenager

Another name for progeria is the "aging disease." This rare congenital disorder affects children shortly after birth often taking their life before they reach twenty. It is a hideous affliction that causes children to lose their hair, teeth, and bone structure. Ten-year-olds look sixty years of age while teenagers resemble senior citizens in nursing homes. Asked to deliver a speech to parents whose children lived with this daily curse, I wondered what kind of message could possibly make a difference for these moms and dads whose "death watch" consumed them.

I arrived early and headed to the hotel conference room to listen in on a "teenage" discussion panel. There were three teens answering questions from an audience of grief-stricken parents. Scanning the forum participants, I couldn't differentiate whether a boy or girl was speaking. Even their voices were victims. One of the moms in the audience addressed a question to the teenager sitting in the middle of the group: "How do you cope with this terrible disease at a time in your life when you should be dating, going to the senior prom, and attending high school football games?" The response from this poor soul gave her sex away. "You know, I've got a choice," she said. "I can choose to complain about my life, or I can look at these handsome young men on my left and right and realize that they look just like me!" Her response got a thunderous ovation. Her humility probably will get her a first-class ticket to Heaven.

I searched for a logical explanation as to how this heart-breaking teenage girl could manage to laugh at her circumstances. Was there something in her genes that gave her the temperament needed to calm the sorrow that filled the room? Did her parents instruct her to put up a good front for the sake of younger progeria-stricken children in the audience? Or was it something else?

The Book of Job tells a story about an innocent man who is tested by God through multiple sufferings. In Chapter 3, verse 20, Job asks, "*Why is light given to him that is in misery, and life to them that are in bitterness of soul?*" Perhaps the answer lies in the hearts of those who are chosen to suffer. As for the rest of us, maybe we can learn from the "Jobs" of this world what happiness is all about. And if we are good students, surely our search will be filled with joy as we come to understand the gifts we have been given.

THROUGH THE EYES OF THE WORLD

Saint Augustine, a fifth-century philosopher, once wrote: "*Where your pleasure is, there is your treasure; where your treasure, there your heart; where your heart, there your happiness.*" Fifteen centuries later the legendary Walt Disney created a cartoon character named Pinocchio whose experience on Pleasure Island gave credence to Augustine's philosophy. Like Pinocchio, we are all subject to temptations that mislead us into thinking that current pleasures ultimately represent true happiness. Instead, these ephemeral treasures too often lead to a broken heart.

There is a great deal of commentary about the seven "deadly" sins and how they individually or in combination with one another, result in the destruction of the soul. Lust, envy, avarice, gluttony, pride, sloth, and wrath are frequently blamed for our failures and embarrassments. No one I know would proudly admit that they couldn't control their passions, jealously, greed, overeating, self-righteousness, laziness, or rage. These "usual suspects" generally receive the blame for why so many people are unhappy. But are these human failings the only adversaries in our search for happiness? Is there another list whose secular pleasures and promises betray our soul?

THE SEVEN SEDUCTIONS

I. Money

There are some poor souls whose birth automatically renders them "untouchable." And too often this designation will remain on their "personal" resumes for the rest of their lives. Conversely, there are others who at an early age discover that they are "heirs" to some fortune that they had nothing to do with. The "haves" and "have-nots" of this world represent two extremes. Those that have wealth generate too much attention, while the poor of this world are long forgotten. For the rest of us, our fate may be measured by how well we handle the "root of all evil."

Money is a funny thing. When we have it we want more of it. When we get more we still never seem to have enough. Ever notice that when people receive raises their satisfaction with the increase seems to fade with each successive check stub? At first they are delighted that they can buy more things, reduce bills, or invest. Other benefits may include new relationships they never had; new pleasures they could never afford; or access to events, people, and places that were once considered beyond their reach. But it doesn't take long before one of two things usually happens: either they realize that extra cash rarely if ever reduces a desire to want more; or they begin to question whether money has any correlation with happiness. If money is the answer to everything, how do we explain the plight of "rich and famous" movie stars, rock stars, professional athletes, and other celebrities whose world is filled with broken loyalties, between them and adoring fans, marriage partners, or business associates? What explanation do we have for the multimillionaire business executives whose greed and deceit too often destroy everything they've built? How can we justify social service agency pleas to "help the poor" but only after management fees and operational expenses are covered? Closer to home, how many parents do we know who do their very best to "buy" their children's love? Unfortunately that love, like after Christmas returns, leaves everybody unhappy. Regardless of our take on the value of money, millions of people every week get in their cars and drive to the nearest lotto outlet hoping to "win" true happiness. After all, if you hit the jackpot wouldn't your troubles be over?

A Tale of Two Winners

Jack won one of the richest lotteries in U.S. history, receiving $113 million AFTER taxes. With that kind of windfall one would think that he was destined to live "happily ever-after." But Jack's luck is not something most of us would ask for. Since he won he has been arrested twice for drunk driving resulting in rehabilitation. Worse yet, his granddaughter was found dead of an apparent drug overdose. All the money on this earth will not bring her back. Other lottery winners have experienced misfortune including lawsuits, suicide, prison time, and dying in poverty. And in one case, the lottery winner's brother tried to have him killed for the inheritance. Their stories are not unique. The next story is.

Debi is also a lottery winner. She didn't win the kind of money others have, ($9 million after taxes), but few deserved to win as much. You see Debi has a little business in California that receives phone calls from the local morgue asking her to pick up abandoned newborns to be buried in her "Garden of Angels" cemetery. Debi told the press that some of her winnings would go to her seven children. The rest would go to her crusade. One can only imagine the day when Debi and her husband meet these children of God for a second time as they enter the gates of Heaven. Maybe one clue to finding true happiness is self-evident: money has no value; what you do with your life does.

II. Beauty

Are beautiful people happier than those who will never be a prom queen, appear on the cover of a well-known magazine, or represent a calendar month? Are happy people beautiful? Some seem to be. For others being attractive too often leads to despair. For both groups beauty is both alluring and temporary. We all would like to have the perfect figure or build, stunning features, and a full head of hair. For guys, that last one may be too much to ask. But you get the point.

The first beauty contest occurs hours after a baby is born. Parents and grandparents crowd around the nursery window to secretly cast their ballots contrasting their child or grandchild with the other contestants. Comparisons never end as infants become toddlers, toddlers become children and children become teenagers. Relatives, neighbors, teachers, coaches, and strangers take license to announce their approval or disapproval of physical characteristics. Society's governing body appears to be members of the media as magazine editors feature beauty tips; designers introduce world famous models prancing down narcissistic runways; television executives parade their "perfect" anchors before the cameras; and Hollywood producers promote their stable of "red carpet" celebrities before, during, and after the show. If that isn't enough, advertising executives bombard the remaining 99.9% of the population with diet and exercise alternatives promising a size six or 33-inch waist; television "makeovers" demonstrate how plastic surgery can improve God's creation; and a host of health and beauty products guarantee to defy nature.

Sex appeal marketing targets all generations. There are "beauty" pageants for children, breast augmentation graduation gifts for teenagers, and "fountain of youth" surgeries for seniors. Though this ugly industry feeds on human vanity, there are some individuals who realize that beauty is a gift from God. They also realize that when this gift is given much will be expected.

Kelly

When Kelly was nine years old, she visited an all-girls school in preparation for fifth grade registration. After spending the day with future classmates, she couldn't wait to get home and tell her mom and dad about the new school. "So, Kelly, how was your day?" her dad asked. "Daddy, I really love the school. The classrooms are really neat and the teacher was very nice," she responded. Kelly went on. "Daddy, I do have a question. Am I pretty?" Wondering where this conversation was heading, her dad queried, "Why do you ask, Kel?" "Daddy, all the girls in the class were really friendly but they kept saying how pretty I am. Am I, Dad?" Her father felt a tinge of sadness that at such a tender age young girls would zero in on the physical attributes of his daughter. "Yes, Kelly, you are a very pretty girl but more important you are a beautiful person." His response tried to hide his discomfort with the topic. "What do you mean, Daddy?"

That question was answered a few years later when this father and daughter were having a conversation about what's important in life. Her dad attended a small Catholic school in Detroit, Michigan, with a graduation class of only seventy-five students. One of those students was a girl named Mickie who had the gift of beauty. But Mickie had something else. She was very kind to her classmates regardless of their athletic ability, grade point average, or popularity in school. Kelly listened intently to her dad as he told her about the day after senior graduation when Mickie, the most popular girl in school, went to every single student hugging and wishing them the best. Kelly pledged to set a similar example.

Through high school and college her maturity and genuine innocence were rarely seen among other girls her age. One Saturday morning as Kelly was shopping in downtown Chicago, a lady approached this twenty-one-year-old and asked: "Would you mind speaking to my producer? Our talent firm has an assignment to find a few models for a series of hair product commercials to air in the fall." The stranger continued, "My producer and I think you may have the 'look' our client is seeking." Kelly spoke briefly with the producer who provided the time and address of the photo shoot. That evening she called her dad for advice. "Daddy, what do you think about this opportunity?" Somewhat concerned her father cautioned: "Kel, before you do anything, make sure this firm is legitimate and the site for the photo session is not in a dangerous area." He said this knowing his daughter had a trusting nature that sometimes led to disappointment.

On the afternoon of the "shoot" Kelly strolled into the studio where she later would report that twenty-five of the most beautiful girls she had ever seen were crowded in the waiting room. Taking her seat next to another girl she waited patiently for instructions. "Who is your agent?" the girl sitting next to Kelly inquired. "Agent? I don't have an agent." Kelly responded somewhat shyly. "Then how did you get in here?" Kelly pointed to the woman orchestrating the process and said, "That lady over there came up to me in a dress shop and asked if I would be willing to come to this photo shoot." "You've been discovered!" the stranger exclaimed. "Here, let me give you my agent's card. He is really good and was responsible for most of the photos in my modeling portfolio." She continued. "By the way, where is your portfolio?" Kelly feeling somewhat out of place smiled and said, "I guess all I've got going for me is my driver's license."

Two weeks later the phone rang and the woman who approached Kelly in the store informed her that she had made the final cut necessitating another session the following day. This time there were only seven girls in the room. Before Kelly was called for the photo session, one of the production assistants walked up to her and said, "Are you a member of the Screen Actors Guild of America?" "What's that?" Kelly inquired. "Oh it doesn't matter anyway because if you're selected you will automatically have to join the union prior to flying out to San Francisco." After the shoot was over Kelly was leaving the studio when the producer walked over and gave her two samples of Dove hair products. That evening Kelly called her mom and dad to update them on the day's adventure. She mentioned the union question and a possible trip to the West Coast. With the same enthusiasm she also expressed her gratitude for the producer who was kind enough to give away "free" hair care products to each finalist!

Neither Kelly nor the producer ever spoke again. To Kelly's way of thinking, the opportunity to participate in a national screening for hair products was both interesting and fun, nothing more and nothing less. After all, how could my daughter be disappointed after receiving enough shampoo to last a month?

III. Intelligence

Who among us would choose to have children whose IQ is thirty points below average? Then again, how many parents do you know wish that their "gifted" twelve-year-old was registered at Harvard University? The ability to learn and reason is what most people need to function in life. Unfortunately, there are many people who are seduced by the belief that superior intelligence guarantees success in today's world. This philosophy can get a lot of people in trouble, especially youth who fail to understand the accountability that comes with "God-given" brains. And when their parents are distracted by honors, awards, and announcements, they too risk disappointment. A common cycle of intellectual despair follows.

Academic challenges usually begin in high school as teenagers find themselves under the G.P.A. microscope. ACT or SAT scores add further pressure. Teachers remind "superior" students that they have a better chance of attending the college of their choice than less "gifted" peers. Parents concur with this assessment pointing out that if the institution their son or daughter goes to is prestigious, the chances for landing a high-paying job after graduation are dramatically improved. And friends confirm what the "bright" student already believes: if you make a lot of money you will be happy. It's so logical. But too often common sense and strong character take a backseat to class rankings, acceptance letters, and scholarship monies. During the competitive "rat race" well-meaning parents get caught up in the conflict as the choice for class Valedictorian generates suspicion.

"My son took harder classes," or "My daughter had harder teachers," are reasons why their child will not be giving the commencement speech. Rejection letters are hidden while acceptance letters are advertised. Eventually all settles down as sons and daughters head off to college in preparation for the future. Sadly for more than a few, five plus years will pass before the proud "graduate" walks across the stage, receives a diploma, and then announces that he or she will be taking a six-week vacation before beginning the job search. Reasons for such a post-graduate decision may include one of the following: 1. They need a break. 2. They need to discover other parts of the world before they are tied down with work. 3. Their mom and dad promised them a trip after they graduated. Months later, many of these degreed intellectuals are still unemployed or underemployed as they take up residence on their parents' couch contemplating why they are so unhappy.

So what happened? Isn't a high intellect a sure roadmap to happiness? If you can't throw a baseball 100-miles-per-hour, receive a six-figure modeling contract, or inherit your father's business, then you've got to rely on your intelligence. What else is there? For most people there's life. And it's what they do with that life that will determine whether or not success is in their future. For some the journey is a circuitous path that builds character and hope. One such story follows.

Project 100,000

During my senior year I had a meeting with the Mother Superior of Saint Rita High School who gently suggested that I learn a trade as college would be a reach. The year was 1966 and the Vietnam War was winding up in Southeast Asia. Realizing that I had little mechanical skills, much less direction, I made the decision to visit with an Air Force recruiter to inquire what opportunities this branch of the military might have for someone who graduated number sixty-first out of seventy-five students. I knew that if the Air Force wouldn't accept me then either the Army or Marines, and ultimately Vietnam would.

"Son," the rather large and physically fit sergeant said, "If you score 80 points on this aptitude test, you can join the United States Air Force." A week later the recruiter called and proudly informed me that I got an "80," right on the button! Three months later a nineteen-year-old was on his way to San Antonio, Texas, to begin basic training at Lackland Air Force Base. One day our unit was ordered to march to an educational facility to participate in classroom studies. Each recruit carried his own personnel file. During a break I noticed that there were only two out of forty airmen whose folders were a different color. One of those selected to carry a yellow folder was me. Curiosity, coupled with questionable courage, demanded that I investigate this oddity further. I walked up to the instructor, stood at attention and asked: "Sir, I was wondering, is there any reason why Airman Jones and I have a totally different folder color than the other thirty-eight airmen?" Looking sternly, the instructor shouted, "You're a *Project 100,000*, now get back in your seat!" One never asked a second question.

After graduating from basic training I received my orders to report to Bergstrom Air Force Base in Austin, Texas, where I learned I was about to be trained as an *Air Operations Specialist*. I remember thinking that the title had a certain ring of "influence." Three months later the *Project 100,000* label would again surface. On a rainy Monday morning I strolled into the base education office. Nearly all my friends were taking college night courses at the University of Texas, and though Mother Superior cautioned against such fantasies, I was confident that I could earn college credits while still on active duty.

"Sergeant Cotter, I would like to apply for funding to take two college courses at the downtown campus." Sergeant Cotter, the base non-commissioned education officer, looked at my application and then opened a large cabinet drawer filled with the files of every enlisted man on the base. As Cotter was looking for my name, I couldn't help notice that a handful of folders were tabbed with the identical color scheme that Airman Jones and I had the honor of possessing during our basic training excursion. Sure enough, the sergeant's fingers stopped on one of the folders with the strange yellow tab. Pulling it out of the drawer Sergeant Cotter looked at me and said: "Oh, you're a Project 100,000." "Yessir. What exactly does that mean?" I inquired realizing that the answer might be somewhat unpleasant. "Airman," Sergeant Cotter continued, "are you sure you want to go to COLLEGE?" After twenty minutes of negotiation I received conditional approval to take only one course with the mandate that a grade of at least a "B" was the price for future financial aid. For the second time I never did get a clear answer to my *Project 100,000* question.

That answer would come three years later with only sixty days left in my tour of duty. One morning while sitting on my bed reading *Time* magazine, there was a small article whose title caught my eye. "**Project 100,000 Program Successful.**" I stood up and began reading feverishly. The mystery was over. *Project 100,000* was a recruiting experiment in which the United States Air Force agreed to recruit 100,000 young men who were NORMALLY NOT FIT FOR MILITARY SERVICE because of physical, psychological, emotional, or intellectual limitations.

"What?" I shouted, hoping no one was in hearing distance. Rereading every category of failure I quickly deduced that the only label that could possibly fit was intelligence or lack thereof. But how was it possible that this staff sergeant, the first in his unit to make the grade in under three years, who handled Air Force One protocols, hundreds of aircraft emergencies including one crash, and the only *Broken Arrow Exercise* in four years, not have the intellect to serve his country? Maybe the Air Force recruiter fudged the score so I could fill Michigan quota requirements. Perhaps Mother Superior was right. Maybe I was not fit for college. Time would tell.

"We Cannot Lower Our Standards."

Two weeks after discharge I returned to Michigan to begin working as a blueprint operator for an automotive division of General Motors. Though I applied for a higher position, I was told that without a degree I didn't qualify. It didn't matter what kind of military experience I had or what my performance was. What mattered was that single sheet of paper. Pride aside, the greater challenge was whether or not I could balance job, school, and home responsibilities, while furthering my education.

For two years I went year-round to college while working fifty hours a week. The schedule was grueling. My marriage was suffering. And the frustration of running a blueprint machine after handling multi-million dollar aircraft emergencies was disappointing. But the day finally came when I earned the title: COLLEGE GRADUATE! This accomplishment led to a promotion and greater promise. Graduate school was next.

After the dean of the business school was finished looking over my application to the MBA program, he looked up and said, "David, I'm sorry, but we can't accept you in the business college because your 2.96 GPA and entrance test scores are below our requirements." "But," I pleaded, "you do realize that I worked and went to school full time while most of your students only attend classes." "Nevertheless," the dean responded, "we cannot lower our standards." "You just did," I replied. And with that, dejected but determined, I immediately walked across campus to apply to the School of Communications where I attended school for another two years to earn a Master of Arts degree. I was flattered when the dean of the graduate program asked if I would consider going on to earn a Doctorate degree. I declined.

My motivation to work and go to school full time for four straight years was driven by my desire to advance myself. But I had other things to prove. Mother Superior was wrong; I should not have been labeled a *Project 100,000* and I could earn my MBA if given the chance.

What I didn't know then that I understand now is that we all at some time in our lives face trials and tribulations that seem unfair. It's how we handle these situations that will ultimately define our roadmap in life. I have since learned something else. Whether your IQ is 100 or 150, you have an accountability to do the best you can, manage your affairs, and accept the Will of God. It would take me several years before I understood this truth.

Another Road Less Traveled

In more cases than not, a person's scholastic ability has little to do with their success in life. High intelligence doesn't necessarily guarantee an easy road for "gifted" students. In my personal experience, I encountered multiple detours before I finally achieved the academic credentials needed to be considered for a more responsible position. Perseverance, confidence, and hard work made up a lot for my poor performance in high school and subsequent inability to score well on tests. But there is another reason why some students succeed in spite of themselves. For these fortunate souls someone in their life set an example of what one must do with what one has been given.

In 1987–88 I had the honor of interviewing over one hundred outstanding families who were selected by National-State-Teachers-of-the-Year. The project was underwritten by Children's Hospital Medical Center of Akron whose leader, Bill Considine, was determined to find outstanding role models for other parents to emulate. One of the reasons why the teachers selected certain families was because of the parents' insistence that their children put a priority on their studies. The following scenarios are representative of what happens when parents demand the best from their children.

Arizona—Kim was fourteen years of age, the younger of two children. Her older brother was a 4.0 student, National Honor Scout, and a guest of the Australian government because of his personal accomplishments. His sister, however, struggled with her studies because of a learning disorder. On the night of her parents' interview, Kim would politely interrupt the conversation with a plea for either Mom or Dad to help her with her homework. This happened on no less than three occasions. After interviewing the parents I asked if I could speak with their daughter alone. Her mother said that Kim was looking forward to the conversation. Mom did caution, however, that I phrase my questions carefully as sometimes her daughter would get confused. After Kim sat down I opened with my usual, "What have been the best and worst of times with your parents?" Kim hesitated, started, stopped again, and finally said: "That question is so hard because my answer is the same." Figuring I failed to listen properly to her mother, I started to break the question into two parts. "No," she said, "I understand your question. You see, the worst of times with my parents is when they insist that I put that extra hour in my studies when all my friends are outside having fun." Kim continued. "But the best of times with my mom and dad is when I'm called up on stage to receive an academic award from the school that my parents were told would be too difficult for me."

Oklahoma—David was the oldest of five children and very popular in high school. One day his mother received a call from the homeroom teacher informing David's mom that her son was very quickly becoming the "class clown." That Friday evening David's mom proudly announced that effective Monday morning, she would be joining David in class the following week and that the empty desk behind his was being reserved for her. "YOU'RE GOING TO DO WHAT?" he inquired. Calmly, David's mom explained that she had heard her son was quite popular and that it was her responsibility to transfer this "talent" to his younger brothers and sisters. Horrified at the prospect of his mother following him from class to class, David begged his mom to reconsider. Sensing desperation in her son's plea she agreed to think it over for a week before she would initiate her plan to "shadow" her son. The following Friday the teacher who had alerted David's mother about her son's behavior called again to inform her that his classroom behavior had taken an unbelievable turn for the better. "It's a miracle" was Mom's reply.

Florida—When a father has a fourth grade education and his wife barely finished eighth grade, you normally don't expect the children to do well in school. But after learning that all five offspring in this home were honor students and that one of them was invited to visit the President at the White House, I had to ask how such academic success was possible. The proud dad shared his secret: "You see, when our children would return home from school, the first thing we all did was sit down and have dinner as a family." The man continued, "When we were finished eating, all my children followed me into the study." I imagined a scene out of the pied piper. The father then said, "Though I couldn't read I still knew our encyclopedia set held a world of knowledge. I would grab one of the volumes, open the book to no particular page, and ask all my children to read to their father." That was it; no special tutoring, computer software, or financial incentives. All he did was set an example and the results speak for themselves.

Rhode Island—National Bunk Day is a time-honored tradition for high school seniors who supposedly earn the right to skip one day of school. For Sonny, the oldest of eight children, this rite of passage was a given; or so he thought. Approaching his mother with confidence, he proudly announced he wasn't going to school the following day because all seniors were allowed to skip class. All she had to do was send a note with any of his younger brothers and sisters stating that Sonny was ill. "You want me to do what?" his mom inquired. Sonny argued that if his mom didn't sign the note that he would be the only high school senior going to class. "Your point?" she retorted. The next day Sonny left for school as he always did. That evening the principal called and asked to speak to Sonny's mom. "Are you telling me that my Sonny never showed up for class today?" she inquired. "Yes, but because it's National Bunk Day all you have to do is tell me his was sick and I'll write an excused absence." "No, sir," came the emphatic response. "My son skipped school and I expect you will deal with his decision!" It was a long weekend for Sonny. The following Monday Sonny came home from school walked up to his mom and said, "Mom, thank you." Suspicious, she looked her son in the eye and said, "For what?" "After the principal told me I had detention for a week he called a special meeting for all seniors." "And?" Sonny's mom inquired. "The principal made this announcement." "Last Friday was National Bunk Day. Parents of three hundred students sent a note to my office saying their son or daughter was sick. One parent told the truth. Her son should be proud of his mother." Sonny told me that story and I have since told many other parents. Hopefully, all of us have learned what conviction can do in our relationship with our children.

I share these vignettes because they taught me two lessons: First, as a parent I have the accountability to do what it takes to inspire my children to do their best in school. And second, if I am successful in this parenting venture, my chances for peace-of-mind in this life and happiness in the next, will be greatly enhanced. The reverse is also true.

IV. Relationships

Is it a question of whom you know? Whom you would like to know? Who knows you? Are "connections" all that important? What about associations with groups, cliques, teams or neighborhoods? One of the most common indicators of whether we are "happy" in life is measured by the relationships we have with others. Members of our family—whether parents, siblings, aunts, uncles, or grandparents—can set an early benchmark as to the influence these "connections" have or will have in our lives. Friends, teachers, neighbors, and coaches can play a significant role in determining how important relationships are in achieving happiness. Co-workers, bosses, customers, and business and community affiliations can positively or negatively impact our degree of contentment. And not to be outdone, spouses and children take center stage when it comes to both the power and importance of relationships. Other influential encounters may come from strangers, celebrities, clubs, cliques, or teams, and an untold number of other souls, whose impact on our life may or may not immediately register.

But are relationships mandatory for one to be happy? I can't think of a single person I know, past or present, that willingly prefers the life of a hermit. On the other hand, why are there so many unhappy people involved in relationships? "Family wars," "broken friendships," "mentor betrayals," "worksite squabbles," and "infidelity" offer a rich curriculum of what not to do. In addition, the media offer an opportunity to observe what price "poor relationships" exact in other people's lives. Can the human family's desperation to be liked and loved result in myopic relationship management? The answer is YES!

Prodigal Parents

Having a good relationship with teenage sons or daughters should be "number one" on every parent's agenda. Unfortunately, in their attempt to be "liked" by their children some parents make bad decisions. Case in point: When a troubled senior in high school asked if she could go on a spring-break vacation to Mexico, her parents said yes. The mother and father's rationale for their decision was based on recent "good behavior" which they felt proved that their daughter would use good judgment even though her boyfriend would be part of the unsupervised group. Result: One pregnant teenager.

Another set of parents gave their son permission to attend a weeklong retreat for high school seniors. At the closing ceremony each student took their turn to publicly tell all the mothers and fathers in the auditorium what their sons and daughters learned and how much their parents meant to them. One young man changed his speech moments before he went on stage. Looking around for his mom and dad he realized that they were not in attendance. In his brief comments to the audience he said, "This retreat made me realize what I need to do to have a better relationship with my parents. Predictably, they are too busy to listen to what I have to say." With that he walked off the stage. That night many happy parents welcomed their sons and daughters home. But for one young man, his estranged journey was about to begin. Result: One broken relationship.

There is no "I" in Team.

The home team was ahead by one run in this fifteen-year-old state championship baseball game that would determine which club would go to the nationals. With only one out away from victory, the batter hit a hanging curveball for a triple. The next batter hit a one-hop ground ball back to the mound where the pitcher cleanly fielded the ball. Instead of throwing to first base to end the game and propel his team into the national spotlight, he tried to throw the runner on third out at the plate. Instead he threw the ball over the head of the catcher which allowed the player to score the tying run. The player who hit the ball back to the mound immediately broke for second base. Now the winning run was in position to end the ballgame. The next batter singled up the middle allowing the player on second to score and end the game. The losing players and coaches were devastated. Their pitcher remained on the mound crying for he knew that it was his mental error that cost his team the championship and the right to represent the State of Ohio in the Nationals. Regardless, every player on his team went up to him and did his best to comfort a fellow teammate. This demonstration was one of the best examples of sportsmanship ever witnessed on the diamond. The boy's father was particularly moved by the compassion his son received. The following year when it came time to prepare the team for the new season, the coaches learned that the same boy whose team stood by him in his darkest hour had chosen to play for a rival team. Result: Broken relationships, broken trust.

Follow the Money Trail

When the corporate construction and acquisition executive of a billion-dollar company came for his first visit to the organization's newest subsidiary, he requested a tour of a parking deck construction site. Standing with the facilities manager he asked how much the project would cost, who the engineering company was, and how the bidding process was handled. Surprised at his questions, the facilities manager responded that the board had approved the project and the local construction firm had a very strong reputation. "That doesn't matter," the corporate executive retorted. "What matters is that MY bonus depends on the success of this project." Result: No relationship, no trust.

In Search of…?

A husband of twelve years and father to three children had just been promoted. The extra income would help make the mortgage payments on their new home located in an up-and-coming subdivision. Hank and Mary seemed to be the perfect couple. Hank was popular with his co-workers and management alike, while Mary was always seen as a loving mother and devoted wife. Life was good. Returning home one Friday afternoon, Hank couldn't wait to begin his weekend with the family. The boys had the usual Saturday schedule of baseball and soccer games, and a picnic was planned after Sunday church services. When Hank pulled in the driveway, he noticed that Mary's car was not in the garage. He thought that his wife was probably picking the boys up from the home of their best friend, who frequently watched the children when Mary had to do some grocery shopping. Entering the kitchen he noticed the one-paragraph letter on the table. "Dear Hank," the formal salutation read, "I'm sorry to have to tell you this but I've decided to leave and search for what will really make me happy. Give my love to our children." It was signed, Mary. That was it. There was no explanation why this mother of three was unhappy, no indication if she intended to return, and no hint as to where she was headed. Result: Broken vows, broken family.

Each of these stories has two things in common: first, a broken relationship; and second, one party being totally surprised by the other. These examples are not uncommon as parent/teen relations are often strained; many athletes put themselves ahead of what's best for their team; poor managers will do whatever it takes to serve their needs; and estranged husbands and wives conveniently forget their wedding vows.

The need for others, like the search for happiness, will never cease. Choose wisely. Failure to do so will only deliver despair and loneliness. And like money, beauty, and intelligence, the value placed on "relationships" is often too high a price to pay.

V. Gratifications

So what happens to those who live paycheck-to-paycheck, are average looking, have trouble calculating the right change from a "Big Mac" purchase, or run with a crowd that most people ignore? Is there no hope? Will the "un-chosen" never find happiness? The answer, according to our hedonistic society, can be found in a variety of pleasures. Chief among these are drugs, alcohol, and sex.

It usually begins with a friend. He offers you some marijuana. It is your first time. What could one little cigarette do? After all, the drug is not addictive; or is it? But then you discover that once the "genie" in the bottle is released there are greater gratifications that must be satisfied. The first time leads to a second time. The harmless puff leads to other temptations that may include ecstasy, cocaine, or heroin. What was once a choice has now become a need. What was once a "happy" feeling is now an unending search for "happiness." In the end, lives, families, and souls are destroyed.

Alcohol abuse has a similar story. The addiction usually has its roots in the home where one or both parents drink in front of their children. When the time is right the youth begins to experiment with beer and liquor. This decision usually leads to greater and greater consumption. From parties to parking lots, the opportunity to drink, get drunk, and indulge in short-term pleasures eventually leads to trouble. Grades are first to suffer. Driven by deceit and rebellion parent/teenager battles are common. If some tragedy or wake-up call doesn't end the madness, the thirst for self-destruction will continue to follow the student to college where a minefield of heartbreak awaits. Binge drinking, drunkenness, and related bad behaviors, are chalked up as a rite of passage. But for many college students, the price to have "fun" will end in disaster. Jail, rape, pregnancy, disease, and even death represent the potential return-on-investment (ROI) for those who succumb to the bottle. And if the disease doesn't get them in college it will get them later in life. Some will lose both their job and career. Others will sacrifice their family. And for more than a few, their health will fall victim to their foolishness.

A third addiction is sex. Temptations are everywhere. Pornography, once scorned, has become the fastest growing industry in the world. Lurid visuals feed the sexual appetite tempting everyone from young children to senior citizens. What was once sacred…what was once forbidden…what was once controlled, is now a cesspool of human depravity. Love has turned to lust. Sex has given way to perversion. And dignity has been replaced by debauchery.

There are other gratifications including food, smoking, and gambling. Even these "pleasures" come with a price. Eat too much and you end up hating the person in the mirror. Smoke and you risk an early death. Gamble and you could lose everything.

If personal gratifications can't promise happiness, perhaps the next seduction can.

VI. *Privilege*

Lady Di was privileged. Mother Teresa was not. One ate with celebrities; the other fed the starving. One dressed for royalty, the other for the forbidden. One was a superstar, the other a saint. Both surrounded themselves with "untouchables." The princess won the hearts of the media; the sister the Nobel Peace Prize. In early September, 1997, the world lost both of these women. At Lady Di's funeral the rich wept. At Mother Teresa's funeral the poor prayed. On whom do you suppose God bestowed the greater privilege?

To be "privileged" implies some sort of immunity from worldly sorrow. Money is no object. Doors are opened. Phone calls are returned. Autographs are requested. Interviews are sought. Life is good. But then it happens. A famous athlete abandons his winning team for additional millions because he "has to feed his family." The following season he ends up blaming fans, the media, and fellow players for his poor performance. Movie stars' "Hollywood" marriage ends months, days, and sometimes hours after the wedding. A politician loses the election because she lost her moral compass. And a "Wall Street" tycoon trades a mansion for a cell because the price of greed must be paid.

Almost every week there is another story about some rich and famous person who reminds the public how happy he or she is. This bliss abruptly ends when the tabloids point out the "star's" lack of judgment, humility, and trust. Perhaps these "privileged" souls should revisit the New Testament's story of a beggar named Lazarus and his encounters with the rich man. After both died it is Lazarus who is now rich while his earthly tormentor suffers in Hell. Maybe the British philosopher Ludwig Wittgenstein, (1889–1951) was right when he said: *"I don't know why we are here, but I'm pretty sure that it is not in order to enjoy ourselves."*

VII. Power

He had everything going for him. He was appointed Treasurer by the most influential man in the country. He was part of the inner circle. Friends, enemies, politicians, military leadership, and respected religious authorities all wanted to speak with him regarding his personal connection. Promises of money, fame, and prestige were laid out before him. All he had to do was say "yes." He did. He died. And his name will live in infamy. His name was Judas Iscariot.

History is filled with characters whose thirst for power led to destruction. Adolph Hitler was responsible for the deaths of over 50 million people. Charles Manson caused the deaths of less than ten. Pontius Pilate will never be forgotten because he ordered the execution of just one man. All three men failed to realize that with the gift of "power" comes the accountability to use that power for the greater good.

Misuse of power can be as simple as pressuring an employee to look the other way or as complicated as board-approved CEO mega-bonuses. The Supreme Court can hand down a ruling that negatively affects millions of citizens, or a rural judge can unfairly sentence a local resident. A national broadcast network can distort a story at the expense of a single public figure, or a small town newspaper editor can ridicule an entire religious denomination. A husband can abuse all his children or a wife, her husband.

Abraham Lincoln once said, *"Nearly all men can stand adversity, but if you're to test a man's character, give him power."* Maybe that's why there is so much talk about "character" but so few examples of it. For those who believe that power will lead to happiness, they would be wise to memorize the following passage. *"For power is given to you by the Lord, and strength by the most High, who will examine your works, and search out your thoughts"* (Wis 6: 2–4).

CHOICE #1
WEALTH or POVERTY

Returning to the Internet, I decided to type in the words "wealth and poverty." Once again the information highway went crazy. Over 40,000 books, tens of thousands of articles, and 31,000 matching sites were at my disposal. With so much wisdom available, I couldn't help but wonder why there are so many people classified as poor or destitute. I suppose if the average person were asked whether they would prefer to be wealthy or poor, 99.9999% would likely choose the former. But if I asked the same population to explain why so many wealthy people are unhappy while a number of people in poverty appear to be happy, I might get a blank look. The world tells us that wealth is a good thing and poverty is to be avoided at all costs. What is not discussed is the "toll" expected from those individuals who pay homage to the "root of all evil."

The Bottom Line

Being wealthy generally refers to how much money you have, the type and number of cars you drive, the portfolio you own, where you live, the trips you take, and who you hang out with. Included with this portrait are certain realities that often inflict the "haves" of this world. Chief among these are:

Relationships—Childhood friends, high school sweethearts, and college buddies are replaced by a new circle of influence.
Security—Backyard picket fences give way to guard dogs, iron gates, and security systems.
Freedom—The opportunity to go for a walk in the park rarely exists.
Time—A "calendar god" ensures that business meetings, social events, and political caucuses take precedence over family matters.
Fulfillment—The desire to increase one's fortune is never satisfied.
Stewardship—Giving of time, talent, or money, without concern for tax implications and public attention, is the exception not the rule.

Temperance—Avoiding excess behavior and lifestyle is a very difficult proposition.
Compassion—Sensitivity towards those in hardship or difficulty is often lacking.
Forbearance—The ability to delay gratification or accept difficult circumstances is seldom manifested.
Faith—Demonstrating the spiritual humility necessary to trust God, while appreciating all His blessings, is an uncommon occurrence.

Even with these handicaps the question must be asked: why are so many wealthy people unhappy? Is their condition driven by some fear that they will lose their fortune? Are they concerned that their children are growing up in a world of "entitlements?" Do they find themselves "buying" relationships? Do they miss being around people whose love of God, family, and country is sincere? Or is it simply that many wealthy men and women, not to mention their sons and daughters, lack the understanding that money does not guarantee happiness? And if that isn't difficult enough, how do they react when they read about poverty-stricken families who appear to be content with their life?

"It's All a Matter of Perspective."

Geoff is a paradox. On one hand he had access to all life had to offer: Handsome appearance, physically fit, athletic, engaging, intelligent, and a successful loving family. But for this 23-year-old, such blessings were not enough. He needed something more. He had to give back before taking what the world would give him. To that end, he accepted a Peace Corps assignment that shipped him off to one of the poorest countries on earth, Gabon, Africa.

Trading New York City with all its noise, chaos, and opportunities, for a silent world of simplicity and poverty, is a culture shock of the highest order. For starters, Geoff was a guest at three funerals the first week he arrived in Mimongo. Malaria is death's calling card for residents of this tiny village located in Central Africa.

For over two years Geoff had the responsibility to teach African children how to speak English. But for this teacher, his class would be unlike any in America. There were seventy-five students: over half had malaria; five had AIDS; and six girls under the age of fifteen were pregnant. Coughing jacks, broken crutches, and labor pains competed with daily lesson plans.

Village life offered additional challenges. Living with a mother and her five children, Geoff had to settle for the same rations allocated to all family members.

The success of the day's hunt determined what was for dinner and how much food there was. It was not uncommon for the family's children to sit next to Geoff to see which child would receive the privilege of "licking" his empty plate. Bathing in a filthy river, sharing quarters with rats and snakes, and exposing his body to parasites, ringworm, and dysentery were daily occurrences. Geoff, like many of his students, also contracted malaria; not once, but twice.

During his tenure Geoff wrote several letters to family and friends. In one letter he said, "Letting 'my children' go wild with magic markers and crayons, let alone plain paper which they've never seen, makes both me and them smile." In another correspondence Geoff reflected, "Reaching my first year anniversary I'm pondering many things." He went on. "I see the malnourished children, stomachs way too wide, literally starving for food. I see our filthiness. I see our bamboo shacks. But then I notice something. Amidst all that poverty I hear laughter. I 'hear' smiling." Geoff continued his teaching. "I see people suffering. I see people starving. But then I see them differently. It really ends up being beautiful. They won't complain. They don't ask for more knowing there is no more to give. They find balance within their souls. THE SIMPLICITY OF THEIR HAPPINESS IS NOTHING SHORT OF ASTOUNDING!"

In the same letter Geoff pointed out how "human touch" transcends any donation, political vote, or good-will package. And with this reality he had the courage to admit: "Something is making these people find joy in something we would find joyless. And though it's tough to find God among such sorrow I now understand that God sometimes hides His answers." Geoff shared additional wisdom. "He hides them in little villages days into the Central African jungle. And it is up to us to find them, no matter how hard that might be. Fortunately for me, I found Him in a little girl's laughter."

The evening Geoff returned to the United States I had the privilege of listening to his story over a beer in a New York City pub. "Geoff," I asked, "what was it like when you had to say good-bye to the people of Mimongo?" The Peace Corps graduate paused a moment and then recounted how the entire village surrounded their "teacher" to pray over him and wish him well on his journey back to civilization. One little boy named Ken took Geoff's hand and said, "Geoffey, please don't leave me. You are my 'Guardian Angel.'"

That night Geoff shared something else. When asked to describe the single most important lesson he learned from his experience, he replied, "Mr. Eich, it's all a matter of perspective."

In the most exciting city in the world there is a young man who understands the difference between hunger and starvation; illness and death; having $10 in your pocket and having no pockets at all. Geoff also understands something else. Happiness is what you make of it. Said another way, the Greek dramatist Sophocles stated: *"Wisdom outweighs any wealth."* Geoff and Sophocles, I suspect, would have made very good friends.

The "A" Team

Wisdom. Experience. Perspective. Does one have to travel half way around the globe before adding these attributes to life's resume? The short answer is NO! Complex wealth and poverty episodes may be staring you in the face; or in my case, three faces.

In the early '80s, one of the most popular television shows was the "A Team" starring George Peppard and a bouncer-like-character known as Mr. T. The plot was the same every week. Some poor underdog needed help against the forces of evil; enter the "A Team" to deliver justice in clever scenarios designed to capture the imagination of young and old alike. Three of the team's greatest fans were my children. Every Tuesday at 7:00 p.m. Robbie, Andrew, and Kelly, would gather in front of the television set prepared to experience another exciting adventure. No other program could compete for their attention; that is until the night I dared to channel surf during the commercial break.

Realizing I had approximately two minutes before Mr. T would return to destroy the villains, I quickly scanned other stations to see what I was missing. Progressing from one program to another, I carelessly paused on a documentary detailing the horrors of the Somalia famine that was ravishing that country. Images of starving children dominated the screen. Gathering my senses I attempted to return to the fantasy world only to be interrupted by the innocent voices of our children. "Daddy, go back," they demanded. "What happened to those children? Why do they look so bad?" they asked. Fumbling with the remote I tried to respond with the voices of their Tuesday night heroes. The children didn't buy it. They wanted answers. "You see," I stammered, "these children come from a land far away and unfortunately they don't have money to buy food." The interrogation continued. "But what can we do to help them, Daddy?" asked Robbie. "Can we send them food?" Andrew inquired. Before I could articulate an intelligent response, the program spokesperson invited "MY" children to feed "HIS" children. "Let's get our piggybanks!" Kelly yelled out. The situation got out of control as my three advocates disappeared up the stairs. Moments later they returned with their "life's savings." Before the night ended, I was writing a check to cover both my children's generosity and my personal shame. Mr. T would have been proud.

The Chamber of the Silent

The actions of our children were driven by a desire to help another child. They didn't consider what they would receive in return. There was no promise of ice cream, staying up late, or an increase in their allowance. They didn't brag about their generosity. In fact, the minute the deal was consummated they immediately requested that Dad flip the channel back to their favorite television show. Maimonides would have approved.

The twelfth-century theologian and physician is the author of a concept known as "The Chamber of the Silent." It seems this Spanish-born Jewish philosopher had a keen understanding about human nature and the gift of charity. Maimonides classified philanthropy according to a person's real intent. His seven degrees of kindness provide a way to measure our compassion.

In the 1st degree one gives with regret. Reluctant benevolence is evident in cases where peer pressure forces an individual to dig into his wallet only because others have done so. When the church collection basket is passed, three different responses usually occur. Some people give what they can the moment they are asked; others pass the basket without making a contribution; and then there are donors whose "sacrifice" is nothing more than a token to avoid attention or to ease their conscience. Another common example occurs when a stranger approaches us for help. To avoid dialogue, we grudgingly respond to the poor man's blackmail. We've all been there.

The 2nd degree occurs when one gives to the sufferer but not in proportion to the need. After attending Mass at Saint Patrick's Cathedral in New York City, I noticed a poor woman standing on the street corner asking for donations. Very few people stopped to offer their assistance. My "Catholic" duty demanded that I pull out my wallet. Walking up to the elderly lady I proudly put ONE dollar bill in her hand. Continuing to stroll down 5th Avenue, I decided to stop in a hotel restaurant for breakfast. Thirty minutes later I paid almost forty dollars for a bowl of cereal, a cup of tea, and a small glass of orange juice. I left a five-dollar tip. That day my "compassion" earned a 2nd degree award. I wonder what that lady ate for breakfast that morning?

When one gives, but not until asked, he or she has achieved a 3rd degree designation. It is always interesting when I hear a fundraiser state that most people are "just waiting" to be asked to contribute to a campaign. I have one question. If the "opportunity" to give is so good, why are they waiting?

The 4th degree is reserved for those whose public giving elicits shame. Any number of publicity seekers may qualify: politicians looking for votes, movie stars posing for the cameras, or, corporate officers enhancing their company's community image. The real attention is on the one who gives, not the one who receives. Though Maimonides was referring to the person in need when addressing who was being shamed, individuals who take advantage of the underprivileged by promoting a personal agenda have embarrassed themselves. In either case, we must aim higher.

When the distressed know their benefactor without being known to him, the latter has entered the 5th degree of kindness. Mother Teresa said it best: "*It is fashionable to talk about the poor. Unfortunately it is not fashionable to talk with them.*"

If the benefactor chooses to remain unknown to those she helps, a 6th degree of kindness occurs. The primary difference between a 5th and 6th degree experience is measured by the donor's rationale for avoiding contact. When one chooses to remain anonymous by not drawing attention to their personal generosity, a higher level of kindness occurs. If however, the real motivation to remain unknown is to avoid uncomfortable conversation with the distressed, then the person writing the check has at best demonstrated a 5th degree example of kindness.

Finally, when deposits are made in secret and the poor remain in secrecy, the benefactor has reached the 7th degree of kindness. This stage is what Maimonides referred to as, "The Chamber of the Silent." During the greatest speech ever recorded, Jesus said, "*But thou, when thou shalt pray, enter into thy chamber, and having shut the door, pray to thy Father in secret: and thy Father who seeth in secret, will repay thee*" (Mt 6:6).

If you accept the premise that, "the more you give, the more you'll get," then you could easily surmise that each degree of kindness has the potential to parallel your final reward. If I choose to "give with regret," then I most certainly will regret the hour I stand before almighty God attempting to explain my behavior. On the other hand, if I practice 7th degree charity, will I not be repaid by the Father in Heaven?

Lady Poverty

In 1181 in the city of Assisi, Italy, a baby boy was born into a wealthy merchant family. The child's name was Francis and one day he would receive the title Saint

Francis of Assisi. Growing up, Francis had everything going for him including money, connections, and a very promising future. But Francis chose another path. Instead of marrying royalty he chose "Lady Poverty" as his bride. In lieu of earning the respect of hundreds of fellow merchants, he inspired over 5000 men to serve the poor. And rather than write "how-to-help-the-poor" operating manuals, he challenged his fellow Franciscans to live by a simple formula: *"Preach the Gospel. Use words if necessary."*

Francis' advice is not reserved for those who wed themselves to poverty campaigns, but to all of us regardless of our walk in life. Whether we run in circles with the likes of Tom Monahan, the Dominos Pizza founder, whose personal desire is to share his fortune with others in need; attempt to raise six children on a mechanics income; or currently reside in Mimongo, we all have the option to do the right thing, at the right time, for the right reason.

In the Gospel of Mark, there is a story about a widow who contributes but two small coins to the temple treasury. Moved by her humility, Jesus said to His apostles, *"Amen I say to you, this poor widow put in more than all the contributors to the treasury. For they have contributed from their surplus wealth, but she, from her poverty, has contributed all she had, her whole livelihood"* (Mk 13: 43–44).

It seems to me that eternal happiness has little to do with the size of our earthly portfolios, and more to do with the resume we present Almighty God at the hour of our death. Whether we are CEOs of Fortune 500 companies, poor farmers in Africa, or somewhere in between, we have the accountability to do our very best with what we have been given. And regardless of what the world says, all of us would do well to listen to the wisdom of Kin Hubbard, who once said, *"It is pretty hard to tell what does bring happiness; poverty and wealth have both failed."*

Something to Ponder

"No people in history have been so richly rewarded with pleasures, and no people in history have been so unhappy." So says Michael D. O'Brien about us in his article *"Modesty in the Culture of Shamelessness."* Though Mr. O'Brien's commentary has more to do with today's fashions than wealth, I couldn't help but notice how applicable his comment was in American society where there are so many unhappy wealthy individuals.

On the other hand, no one should draw a direct correlation between wealth and happiness, or for that matter, unhappiness. Tom Monaghan, founder and past CEO of Dominio's Pizza, is a very wealthy man. But his affluence has little to do with the size of his portfolio and everything to do with the size of his heart.

Since he sold his company, Tom has personally invested millions of dollars toward the development of a Catholic University and entire community in Florida. His generosity knows no bounds.

If there is any relationship between wealth, poverty, and happiness, it is simply based on how the individual handles what he or she has been given. In the Book of Proverbs 22:2, it is written, *"Rich and poor have a common bond: the Lord is the maker of them all."* And in this verse there is hope. For it doesn't matter if you are born wealthy or poor, wise or simple, healthy or sick. What does matter is what you do with your life. To make this point, consider the implications behind the following line from scripture: "Wealth is good when there is no sin; but poverty is evil by the standards of the proud" (Sir 13:23).

It seems to me that God simply wants all mankind to do good. Some of us are blessed with untold material gifts, while others find blessings in poverty. In either case, both groups have their calling. And both groups will answer to their Creator at the end of their lives.

As an exercise, I invite you to imagine that you are standing outside the gates of Heaven when suddenly an angel appears. Imagine further that admittance to paradise is dependent upon how you answer the angel's questions. How would you respond to, "If money buys happiness, what buys eternal happiness?" "If Hell exists, what would you charge for an admission price?" "If you had the power to decide who gets into Heaven, how comfortable would you be turning the earthly poor away?" And finally, "Why do you suppose the 'King of kings' was born in poverty?"

There is another question that ultimately you will have to answer. "Did you make a sound investment in your search for eternal happiness?" As you consider your response, remember that the choices you make in this world will determine the choice God makes in the next. Said another way, "Material abundance without character is the surest way to destruction" (Thomas Jefferson).

CHOICE #2
SELF or OTHERS

Thank You, Clarence

In 1946 there was a story circulating around the country about a man named George whose life was filled with both happiness and despair. One moment things were going well, and the next moment everything went to "hell." He was ready to go off to college, when his dad suddenly died. He was preparing to leave on his honeymoon, when he got word that the family business was about to go under. When his younger brother Harry signed a contract to work in another city, George was forced to cancel his plans to go to college. After his uncle misplaced a large sum of money from the family's Savings and Loan, George realized that his own relative would be arrested for embezzlement. This "last straw" nearly pushed him to suicide. Enter Clarence.

Clarence was George's Guardian Angel, assigned the responsibility of educating his student about what was truly important in life. While in deep despair, George made a remark that "he wished he had never been born." Clarence used this opportunity to show George what life would have been like had he never existed. George soon discovered that the brother he saved from drowning would have died because George was not there to rescue him; that his boss, the town's pharmacist, would have landed in prison because George wasn't there to avoid a fatal prescription error; Mary, George's wife, would have ended up an "old maid" because George wasn't alive to court, and eventually marry her; and his uncle would have become an alcoholic and the family business would go bankrupt, because George was not there to manage both. After George witnessed all the good he had done in life, he cried out to God, "Let me live again." Such is the story of the Christmas classic *It's A Wonderful Life*, starring Donna Reed, as Mary, and Jimmy Stewart as George Bailey.

Imagine if God wrote a new creation script giving each one of us the opportunity to observe what our lives would be like before we were born, and the choice to accept or reject our earthly commissions. Do you think that He would tempt us with fame, fortune, love, or some other worldly enticement, in order to get us in the birth canal? I don't. I believe He would make us an offer we couldn't refuse, promising eternal joy if we simply love others as He loves us. Regardless of our imagination, the reality is this: God gives us a choice. We can spend all our energy on what we think will make us happy, or we can bring a little happiness to others. The following stories demonstrate why the latter is the better choice.

For Others

Saint Maximilian Kolbe is a portrait in "servant leadership." The story of how he gave his life for another has been told in both book and film. As a Polish Catholic priest he found himself branded as prisoner "16640" in the dreaded Auschwitz concentration camp. When the Nazi Commandant threatened to murder ten men in retribution for the escape of a single prisoner, one condemned man begged that his life be spared. Just when the officer was about to reject his plea, Fr. Kolbe stepped forward asking to take the place of the prisoner who begged for mercy. Startled, the Commandant quickly granted the wish of the Catholic priest who, with nine others, was led off to die in a starvation bunker.

Throughout the history of the United States Armed Forces, similar examples of self-sacrifice have been recorded in the annals of war. Almost 3500 men and one woman have received the *Medal of Honor*, given to military personnel whose heroic action was recognized as beyond the call of duty. Stories of soldiers falling on live grenades to save their buddies, carrying wounded men to safety during murderous enemy fire, or staying behind to fight overwhelming odds so that others could escape are recorded so that we may never forget the sacrifice these heroes made.

But does one have to "die" to be both remembered and admired? Gerry Faust achieved both honors simply by demonstrating a servant's heart. He was appointed the 24th head football coach for the University of Notre Dame on November 25, 1980. In his position he was expected to act a certain way around players, alumni, and fans. But Gerry was different. He personally cleaned up the locker room after the game. He helped many players on and off the field who only needed someone to listen to their problems. And he often immersed himself in the needs of campus students who required direction in their lives. Everyone liked Gerry for who he was, not how many games he won. Eventually, Gerry's win/loss record cost him his job. In the eyes of many sports pundits, Gerry was a loser. But for those who knew the character behind the man, they could only echo what television personality Regis Philbin wrote after Gerry lost his coaching position: *"Gerry Faust will tell you he may not have been the right coach for Notre Dame, but he was the right man. He still is."*

Whether Catholic priest, military hero, or football coach, each story is a compelling example of what it means to disregard personal well-being or glory, for the sake of others. But sacrifice, big or small, has its merits. The only difference between parents who adopt twelve children, and those who adopt two, is the size of the family. A volunteer who donates fifty hours a year to her favorite cause, is no less valuable than another caregiver who shares her time three full days a month. And there is no charity on earth that will refuse a monetary donation because it's too small. Furthermore, the "gift of giving" is measured by the satisfaction one receives for serving others. Even children understand this principle.

The Christmas Present

Sherry was the very "spirit" of Christmas. From decorating the entire house, to wrapping all the gifts, to baking dozens of cookies, it was Mom's time to celebrate the holiday season with her husband and six children. Unfortunately during one Christmas season, Sherry was suffering from a severe back injury necessitating multiple painkillers and mandatory bed rest. As December 25th approached, this loving mother became more and more depressed as she felt she was letting her family down.

On Christmas Eve, Dad called his children together around the "poorly" decorated tree. "Look kids," he started, "Mom is very sad because she can't do what she has always done for us at Christmastime." He went on. "I think our job is to bring Christmas to your mother." A plan was crafted to be executed the moment Mom fell asleep. Tommy the oldest, would join his sister Mary in taking all the decorations off the tree. Maggie would bring the disc player and Christmas music up to Mom's room. David would help Dad carry the tree up the stairs. Mandy had the responsibility to bring up all the gifts while Teri followed with Dad's version of holiday cookies.

Two hours later everything was in place. The tree was covered with bulbs, garland, ribbons, and lights. The manger scene was set up on the dresser table. Presents were competing for bedroom floor space. Candles were lit while *Silent Night* was softly playing. The children positioned themselves around Mom's bed, quietly waiting for her to awaken. Dad stood off in the corner, moved by the outpouring of his children's love for their mother. The candle's almond scent and beautiful Christmas carol had their effect as Sherry began to arouse from her slumber. Almost in unison the children whispered, "Merry Christmas, Mom."

This greeting was followed by Dad's emotional, "Merry Christmas, Honey." That night a very special mother discovered how much her family loved her.

A few years later this wonderful family was interviewed for a book on parenting. When the children were asked, "*What was the best of times with your Mother?*" They cheerfully responded with, "It was the year we gave Mom Christmas." They didn't mention anything about what *they* received for Christmas. There was no discussion about a special family vacation, or year-round things their mom did for them. All they could talk about was the time they gave something special to someone special. And without a doubt, the greatest gift received that Christmas Eve was the love these children gave to both of their parents.

All About Me

Unfortunately, too many people fail to understand what it means to put others above self. Every time I see a Nike commercial, or recognize the "swoosh" on college and professional athletic uniforms, I'm tempted to ask what "Just do it" means. Is this popular phrase a subliminal message, promising some sort of happiness for taking action regardless of intent or consequences? Does the campaign's theme parallel sitcom and soap opera programming, whose actors and actresses affirm that, "everybody does it"? And is there a conspiracy by Hollywood magazines to report on the latest celebrities who, "just did it"? Are these pleasure-seeking suggestions representative of a world too caught up in the image of "self"? From self-esteem, to self-help, the ME generation, once a product of the '70's, has returned in the 21st century.

With slogans like, "we deserve a break today," is it any wonder that too much attention is focused on our personal needs and wants? Maybe that's why so many service clubs are losing membership, hospitals are scrambling for new volunteers, and organizations like *Big Brothers and Big Sisters* experience financial shortfalls.

But before I become too cynical about three little words, ("Just do It"), perhaps I should take a more positive approach to the power of the invitation. Florida's Kay O'Bara ignored the press, her friends, neighbors, and doctors, who all agreed that she should let her comatose daughter die. For over thirty years she has cared for Edwarda, twenty-four hours a day, seven days a week, 365 days a year. Anne Sullivan never gave up on her blind and deaf student, Helen Keller. Ms. Keller later became an internationally famous author and lecturer. And at the Seattle Special Olympics, during the 100-yard-dash event, eight contestants stopped running halfway down the track when they realized that one of their competitors had fallen. Returning to help the little boy to his feet, all nine children linked arms and walked across the finish line. Kay, Anne, and nine Special Olympic champions would probably agree that the phrase, "Just do it" has its place when it comes to serving others.

"He Ain't Heavy"

One of the most moving scenes in Mel Gibson's *The Passion of the Christ* is when Simon of Cyrene puts his arm around Jesus to help Him carry the cross. The camera angles highlight the two of them trudging up the hill of Calvary like two brothers preparing to die together. The image was an exclamation point to Jesus' parable about *The Good Samaritan* (Lk 10: 29–37). In that story a stranger was moved with compassion for a man who was stripped and nearly beaten to death. Not only did the Samaritan tend to the injured man's wounds, but he offered to pay an inn keeper to care for the patient until he returned.

Jesus "walked the talk." He gave sight to two blind men in Jericho. He cured the centurion's dying servant. A deaf and dumb man was healed in Sidon, near the Sea of Galilee. Demons were cast out of a possessed man and demoniac child. At the request of a synagogue ruler, the "prophet" brought a little girl back to life. He did the same for Lazarus. Lepers were cured, withered hands were straightened, cripples walked, and condemned souls were forgiven.

It didn't matter whether the person in need was a relative, friend, enemy, or stranger. What mattered was that someone needed help. There was no reward for kindness. No lawyer, high priest, or Roman officer testified that Jesus exemplified what it meant to "love one's neighbor." And there is no record of any apostle mentioning anything about the relationship between earthly altruism and eternal happiness.

So why do it? Why go the extra mile to help someone you don't know? Why reach out to others at the expense of your personal time, talent, or treasure? What's in it for you? The answer may lie within the human spirit. For some, it may be guilt; for others, conscience; but for most, people help others because they want to.

Someone rushes into a burning house to save another. When asked why he took the risk, the answer is often, "Anyone else would have done it." Organizational leaders take pride in their volunteer-of-the-year, who is paraded before the cameras. In more cases than not, the award winner begins the acceptance speech by humbly stating that it was an "honor" to give back. Parents who choose to adopt handicapped children often remind other moms and dads that it is a "blessing" to care for the less fortunate. Benefactors who leave a significant portion of their estate to their favorite charity, only confirm what others knew about the deceased.

At the end of the day, most of us serve others for two reasons: one, it is the right thing to do; and two, there is a sense of satisfaction knowing that the choice we made is responsible for the inner peace we feel. Those who serve others tend not to calculate what they will get back if they do something right. And rarely, if ever, will you hear anyone postulate about earning one's way to Heaven because of the "credits" they have earned on earth. On the contrary, those whose humanitarian gestures are natural, truly understand the meaning of the phrase, "*When much is given, much will be expected.*" And in the silence of their hearts, nothing else is required.

Leadership

I have had the honor to work with several men and women whose leadership style and skill represent all that's right in serving others. Two individuals stand out.

One is a lady named Helen Hoesing who faced a formidable challenge. As the new Vice President of Nursing for a major mid-western hospital, she was responsible for over 700 clinical professionals. Her first challenge was to address a serious morale problem among nursing ranks. The first day she started her new position, Helen called in her executive assistant and requested that over the next ten days, every supervisor be scheduled thirty minutes to personally meet their new nursing officer. Around-the-clock meetings were held with over eighty personnel. No conversation was off limits. Some nurses shared their anger, others cried, and most opened up about what was right and/or wrong about the organization. Within two weeks this remarkable woman had gained the respect of the entire nursing workforce.

There were a number of reasons for her success. Helen listened. Helen was professional. And Helen had a great sense of humor. But perhaps her greatest gift was her ability to recognize the importance of "servant leadership." She understood that to earn the respect and loyalty of those she was accountable for, she must be willing to do whatever was necessary to get the job done. Whether dressing up as a "gorilla" on Halloween to entertain the entire management team; revamping a decades-old emergency nursing protocol in twenty-four hours to improve patient care; or quietly manipulating male-dominated leadership for the right reasons, Helen's calling was, like any good nurse, to serve others.

In challenging times Helen would find a way to put life in perspective. When her home was robbed, she found humor in the fact that among the many valuable objects lost, the thieves also stole her "favorite" broom. On another occasion, Helen and a fellow hospital administrator were driving in a torrential rainstorm when she suddenly pulled over to the side of the road laughing uncontrollably. Her passenger asked, "Helen, what's so funny?" Helen could hardly get the words out as she held on to the steering wheel while intense rain pelted the windshield. Finally, through tears of hysterical laughter, she said, "I'm the 'lady' who just ran out of gas, and you're the 'gentleman' who understands that it's your duty to walk to the service station." I nearly drowned that morning.

Another leader I had the honor of knowing taught me the importance of putting things in order. Bill Considine is the CEO of a major Children's Hospital in Akron, Ohio. When his office called to invite me to meet with him for an executive position on his staff, I immediately prepared my "portfolio" listing accomplishments that I was sure he was looking for. I had strategic planning documents, market share reports, advertising samples, and various product plans, all of which represented typical skill sets needed to function as a Vice President of Marketing and Planning.

Bill met me in a hotel lobby where we found a quiet lounge to begin the interview process. He opened with the usual question. "So, David, tell me a little about yourself." Grabbing my resume package, I started to conduct my "show and tell" segment which I was sure would qualify me for the position. Five minutes into my performance, Bill gently interrupted me. "David," he began, "I believe your background is compatible with the needs of our hospital. But what I'm really interested in is how you spend time with your family, what you do for your community, and what's important in your life."

If I had said that I was responsible for increasing market share ten percent at a cost of sharing less time with my family, the interview would have been over. If I had communicated every detail in an award-winning advertising strategy, but failed to describe my volunteer involvement, Bill would have sent me packing. And if I had analyzed my strategic planning process, with all its business acumen, but couldn't articulate life's priorities, I would never had spent ten years under the tutelage of one of the best known child advocates in the country.

An additional point is worth noting. Before Bill offered me the job, he asked that my wife Cindy fly out to Akron to meet her husband's future boss. When Cindy returned two days later, I asked her what she thought about Bill Considine. Cindy looked at me and said, "I don't know if Akron is a good place to raise a family, or if Children's Hospital is a good place to work; what I do know is that Bill loves children and the family, and that can't be all bad." As I look back on my interviewing experience, it's clear to me that Bill was looking to hire a husband, father, and child advocate. And should that person have some background in marketing so much the better.

Henry Drummond, a nineteenth-century Scottish evangelist and author, once said, "*Half of the world is on the wrong scent in the pursuit of happiness. They think it consists in having and getting, and in being served by others. It consists in giving and serving others.*" Bill Considine and Helen Hoesing have been on the "right side of the world" for many years. And because of people like them, the world is a better place.

Katrina

The images told the story. Mothers and fathers clinging to their children as they boarded busses to some unknown destination; elderly residents wandering flooded streets; stranded pets seeking dry land; police officers trying to enforce law and order; firemen desperately trying to stop entire neighborhoods from burning down; volunteers going house to house searching for hurricane victims; hospital personnel struggling to keep the generators going so that their patients would live; scenes of destruction, courtesy of massive television coverage and magazine photographs; and unbelievable sorrow in the faces of tens of thousands as they struggled to survive the aftermath of America's worst natural disaster.

Many citizens blamed local and national governmental authorities for reacting too slowly. Some politicians blamed members of the opposing party implying that had they been in power, things would have been different. And media personalities did everything they could to infuriate the American people, as they sat in the comfort of their national television studios conducting numerous "witch hunts." Some of their targets were police officers who abandoned their duty to see if their own families were alive.

Disease, death, and despair riddled the nation's heart. But something else caught our attention. The sight of joy on the faces of first responders who rescued a child from certain drowning, gave us hope. Volunteers from all over the country feeding thousands of homeless victims, animals, and exhausted police, military and firemen, gave us a sense of pride. And thousands of national, state, and local organizations that led a "call to action," gave us the opportunity to serve others in need.

Like most Americans, I was glued to the television set waiting for the nightly news to send me visuals of human suffering. Daily newspapers supported the ghastly images with a blow-by-blow description of the tragedy. And talk show hosts added their "two-cents" worth of commentary designed to guarantee their network's ratings. Yet nothing impacted me more than a series of emails written by a military officer who described the horror facing the people of New Orleans. From floating bodies to shipwrecked vessels, from garbage to stench, from human cesspools to human suffering, this soldier saw it all.

But he saw something else. While wading into a chapel, his attention was drawn to a painting that was above the altar. It was a picture of a man hanging on to a wooden cross in the middle of a raging sea. The image was a powerful reminder that in times of peril, man's only hope is God. And through God there will be many, like the officer who saw the picture, who will one day be able to answer the question: "But when did I see you, Lord?"

Something to Ponder

Is it possible to be both selfish and happy? Can a person continually ignore the needs of a neighbor, friend, child, coworker, or even stranger, while at the same time experience contentment in life? Anyone who believes that happiness has nothing to do with stewardship is at best delaying the sorrow that lies ahead. The following commentary and corresponding questions are designed to challenge your thinking.

- Most of us have met one or more individuals who touched our heart, conscience, or soul, in such a way that they made a significant impact on our lives. For me, it was Sergeant Wheeler. He loved his work and he loved baseball. One day he left the base to drive downtown where one of his staff was scheduled to pitch for the Air Force team. Most of our players were white. The team they were playing was an all-black club from Austin, Texas. Sergeant Wheeler was our loudest supporter cheering the base team to victory. After the game I asked him why he was so vocal, given that he was the only black man in the stands clapping for the white pitcher on the mound. He simply responded, "David, you saw the game as a contest between 'black and white.' I saw the game as a contest between two good ball clubs. Sergeant Wheeler taught me to never let skin pigmentation determine the consequence of any encounter. Looking back, can you identify special individuals that touched your heart in such a way that you now have the accountability to touch others?

- When I interview final candidates for a particular position, I always end the discussion with the following question: "Please list in order of priority the five most important things in your life and why." Can you list yours? Why did you choose this list and why did you put them in the order you did? Said another way, does your list represent what you believe will make you happy? Furthermore do you believe that by focusing your life's attention on these five priorities, you will achieve eternal happiness?

- Imagine for a moment that there is no Hell, only Heaven. How happy would you be, sharing paradise for all eternity with souls who were so narcissistic that they had no time, desire, or compassion to help others?

- Can you explain why the "human heart" responds better to kindness than it does to coldness? Can you ever recall a time in your life when you enjoyed being around someone who couldn't care less about you? If not, why would you choose to be around those whose excuse for bad behavior is that they just wanted to be happy?

- Take a moment and list all the individuals in the past one hundred years that you believe define a hero. Next to your list jot down the qualities that you feel were reasons why these role models set the bar for the rest of us. How many of these traits do you have? And what do you think are the chances of finding souls in Heaven who have similar attributes?

The choice before you is whether you go through life wanting to be served, or finding it in your heart to serve others. And should you have difficulty deciding which road to take, I invite you to memorize the following passage:

"Then the king will say to those on his right. 'Come, you who are blessed by my Father. Inherit the kingdom prepared for you from the foundation of the world. For as I was hungry you gave me food, I was thirsty and you gave me drink, a stranger and you welcomed me, naked and you clothed me, ill and you cared for me, in prison and you visited me.' Then the righteous will answer him and say, 'Lord, when did we see you hungry and feed you, or thirsty and give you drink? When did we see you a stranger and welcome you, or naked and clothe you? When did we see you ill or in prison, and visit you?' And the king will say to them in reply, 'Amen, I say to you, whatever you did for one of these least brothers of mine, you did for me.'" (Mt 25: 34–40)

CHOICE #3
QUALITY or QUANTITY

It's All About Time

I once interviewed a young man named Jason, who was about to graduate from high school. Since the discussion centered on the importance of time in the parent/teen relationship, I asked him what he thought about the phrase "quality time." He laughed and told me that the issue in his family was not *quality*, but *quantity*. He then told me this story. When he was fifteen his mom and dad promised to buy their son a car for a graduation gift if his grades met their expectations. After three years of stellar academic performance, he approached his parents to see when they could all go to the local auto mart to shop for his new wheels. Sadly, Mom and Dad informed Jason that his father had been laid off from his job, and unfortunately the car purchase would have to be postponed. I asked Jason how he felt about their broken promise. His response is the impetus for this chapter. "Mr. Eich," he said, "when my parents told me of their decision I was disappointed. But when I saw how sad they were, I knew it was my responsibility to remind them how grateful I was for their greatest gift—time."

I asked Jason to explain. "You see," he said, "all my friends have parents that have showered material gifts on their children. But when it came to spending time with their sons or daughters, they were frequently too busy." Jason went on. "My mom and dad were always at my games, always had time to help me with my studies, and always listened to what I had to say about my day, my world, my life, my dreams. They were never too busy for me." His final comment spoke volumes. "Today's young people don't want 'quality' time from their parents. They want 'quantity' time. If that happens, 'quality' will follow."

I shared Jason's wisdom with my wife, Cindy. And though Robbie, Andrew, and Kelly, were ten, eight, and five, respectively, we knew that our decision to sacrifice our personal time for the needs of our children was the right choice. We both recognized that our sons and daughter would grow up very quickly, and "time" was too precious to take for granted. More and more parents thought our parenting style was old fashioned because we were uncomfortable scheduling dates, dinners, events, and conversations with our kids. One mother told us in so many words, that to be happy we must first please ourselves. This was the same lady who complained that she would not be able to join her husband in Hawaii, because her seven-year-old son fractured both arms in a playground accident.

Advice can be a welcome resource when it comes to raising children. It can also serve to mislead young parents who have yet to experience their true "calling." Examples of both follow.

Warning: It Only Gets Worse

When Cindy was pregnant with our son Robbie, well-meaning friends, relatives, and co-workers did their best to prepare the parents-to-be for the trials and tribulations that lay ahead. Brutal descriptions of sleep depravation, nuclear-waste diapers, and colic "madness" were mixed with promises that such experiences only last a short time. But how do you handle parenting pressures when your son's sleeping patterns can't tell the difference between the sun and the moon, his brother doesn't sleep through the night for two years, and their little sister's colicky condition leads to special medication for their mother? The promise of "this too will pass" couldn't pass soon enough.

But pass it did, only to be greeted by the "terrible twos." This is the era when the children become household explorers capable of destroying every inanimate object within their grasp. Our son Andrew was in charge of the "pot and pan" symphony and building a toy obstacle course. Robbie entertained his mother by squeezing all his food in his little hands until he was satisfied that the distance between highchair and floor made his "bombing mission" worth the effort. And Kelly had the curious habit of taking off her diaper just when #2 was about to arrive.

Friends and grandmas assured us that our children would reach a time when they could ride the school bus alone, go on sleepovers, and negotiate for higher allowances. But with this maturity came the first challenge to our parental authority. For Robbie it was egging a neighbor's house. During the same incident, he stood guard while his friends used a pellet gun to shoot the windows out of a car that was under wraps. Andrew did better. He took the same pellet gun to school to show his friends. Thank God his indiscretion occurred seven years before Columbine. As for Kelly, her independence was confirmed the evening she came downstairs to model her new haircut. The only problem was she forgot to cut the other side of her head! She was six years old.

Final warnings arrived the day we officially entered the "teenage years." We were told to prepare for open hostility, lying, and any number of parental heartbreaks. Oh, there was one drinking episode, two cracked up cars, and the occasional challenge to our authority. But when I look back, those teenage years may well have been some of the best times Cindy and I had with our children.

What many of these well-intentioned friends didn't prepare us for was the day our grown-up sons and daughter would trot off to college. This was a time of sorrow as we realized that the hour had come for us to let go of what we loved most—our children. We would have gladly relived all the sleepless nights and empty checkbooks, in exchange for never having to say goodbye. So with all the tears and frustrations, not to mention expense, how is it that we refer to this period of our lives as some of our fondest memories? And what does this parental experience have to do with happiness? The answer begins with the most important person in our family: Mom.

A Mother's Heart

It's hard to explain. A mother gets up in the middle of the night at the slightest sound, races into the baby's bedroom to make sure all is well, then refuses to go back to sleep if a diaper is dirty, a mouth is hungry, or a child must be rocked. A few hours pass, and eventually this exhausted mother falls asleep only to surrender to the demands of an obnoxious alarm clock. Day-after-day, week-after-week, month-after-month, Mom faces the daunting task of caring for her child, her husband, her home, and sometimes her sanity. The daily "patience" antidote usually comes in the form of an infant's smile or a baby's laugh. One minute a mother is nearing frustration, and the next she is basking in the glow of her resting child. The paradox doesn't stop there.

As the child grows, mom's schedule does also. There are school lunches to make, clothes to clean, busses to catch, meetings to attend, sporting events to watch, doctors to visit, meals to fix, games to play, lessons to teach, and phone calls to return. And these activities don't even consider the few moments she requires for her personal needs, time with her husband, and conversations with friends, neighbors, or relatives. Working, shopping, cooking, and cleaning generate additional pressures. The "motherhood repertoire" repeats itself over and over again with each additional child.

As the years go by, teenage independence enters the scene. Mom returns to restless nights as her son or daughter is with friends she doesn't know, in a car she doesn't own, on its way to a place she's never been. Concern is never far from her state of mind, whether awake or asleep. And though high school gives way to college and college to career, a loving mother never stops worrying about her children.

For my wife, Cindy, daily calls from a loving daughter, and weekly calls from loving sons, provide a moment of joy. Too often that "moment" is replaced by concern over the safety and health of her children, now adults themselves.

But if you asked this mother of three if raising children with all its challenges was worth it, she would respond with a resounding YES! No doubt there were memories she would rather not drudge up: three-year-old Robbie waving goodbye to his mom as the nurse was wheeling her first-born into surgery; contracting the flu when her husband was out-of-town while three young children were crying for attention; or having to take a door off its hinges after Andrew locked himself in the bathroom no fewer than three times within one hour.

Cindy would also admit that there have been times when joy and happiness were replaced with anger and despair. But through it all, she understands that God did not bless her with Robbie, Andrew, and Kelly so she could be happy. On the contrary, her primary responsibility was to love and care for her children while protecting them from evil. She has done that. And her success as a mother in this world will have a whole lot to do with her happiness in the next.

A Father's Commitment

As the primary income-earner, I had the responsibility to make sure we could meet our financial obligations. Unfortunately this "positioning" statement is a poor excuse for failing to be both a good father and a loving husband. Fortunately my wife made sure I took the right "courses" to achieve both.

Initial fatherhood coursework includes: how to wipe your child's bottom; how to boil a bottle; how to give a bath; how to protect your shirt and tie when "burping" the baby; how to lift the "sleeping" darling out of the swing so that mom won't be up half the night; and my favorite, how to remove "vanilla pudding" from your child's hair.

After fathers have passed "parenthood 101," they are promoted to "parenthood 202." In this course, Dad learns how to chase a naked two-year-old around the house, as the child deposits diarrhea on the new carpet; how not to assemble toys, baby carriages, and any assorted contraption that purportedly was designed for non-mechanically inclined males; and when to listen to your wife about "her" bad day.

The third course begins when your daughter wants you to play "house" and your sons insist that ten-hour-plus workdays, are no excuse for not playing ball. This curriculum often includes requests to coach the team, attend the recital, and get up each morning at 5:30 to help with the 200-customer paper route. Other requirements include teaching your daughter that there is no such thing as "forty-one o'clock," or your sons that there are consequences for not hustling on the ball field.

During adolescent years, fathers must set the standard for respecting mothers. Other accountabilities include teaching your teenager what evil awaits them should they "forget" to help around the house; that learning to drive, like school field trips, are privileges; and forgetting their mother's birthday is too high a price to pay.

When it's all said and done, a man's commitment to his role as father and husband serves only to make this world a better place. And one day, I will stand before almighty God to account for what I have done or failed to do. At that hour, I hope to hear the words: "Well done, good and faithful servant, for I blessed you with a loving family, and as you have loved them, so have I loved you. Welcome home."

Friends

Though Cindy and I would like to take credit for all the good things our children have done, we must rightly share the honor with other parents whose commitment to their children mirrored our own.

Buzz and Patti have two wonderful children. Their son and daughter work hard. They give back. They respect their mom and dad. They honor their grandparents. They are model citizens who will make a positive difference in their community. And all it took was time; time to be at every school function when other parents were too busy; time to volunteer for countless charities, or coach soccer, baseball, and basketball teams, when other adults were tied up with more important things; time to teach their children right from wrong, good from evil, instead of letting society prepare life's lesson plans; and time to challenge their children to do the very best they could, without worrying about "self-esteem," "public image," or what other friends and neighbors thought.

Larry and Sue have three children. Like Buzz and Patti, they are blessed. Their "sense of humor" was especially appealing. Sue would affectionately remind Cindy and me that our son Andrew was a great kid followed with, "Thank God he's yours." Larry was the only coach I had the honor of working with, who could laugh during thirty-mile-an-hour winds, temperatures dropping below forty degrees, and torrential rains, all of which contributed to our team's demise in the championship game. We lost. I nearly froze to death. And Larry laughed.

Rich and Jan provided both Cindy and me countless hours of "adult" discussion. Jan and Cindy entertained each other as they walked two miles every day talking about everything from education to shopping habits. Rich and I exchanged philosophies on politics, religion, sports, books, movies and a litany of other topics. Since their son and daughter were frequent playmates of our children, the opportunity to collectively share parenting "war stories" was ever present.

There were other moms and dads and their children who came into our lives. Baseball parents shared a common bond as our sons battled on the diamond. School parents rallied with us, as issues involving academics, and/or raising money, needed attention. Neighborhood parents surfaced when children would go from house-to-house to play with others their age. When it came to sharing and growing together, these colleagues represented all that was right with parenthood. We needed them as much as they needed us. Our children trusted these adults. Their children trusted Cindy and me.

Looking back, our common thread was time; not quality time; quantity time. Heck, we were all too busy to "schedule" dates with our children, much less our friends. But we were never too busy to recognize what was important in life and to appreciate that friends who believe as we did, made it so much easier to raise our children. In a strange way the friendships we had paralleled the friendships our children had. Our sons and daughter knew whom not to hang around with, in part because of the relationships we had with our friends, and they with their children. A standard was set. A trust was formed. A bond was created. And even today, when phone calls are exchanged, the first question out of the mouths of these mothers and fathers is, "how are the kids?" Every question that follows pales in comparison. It has always been that way. It will always be that way.

The "Twelve" Gifts

In an earlier chapter I mentioned that I was involved in a project to recruit and interview over 100 families from around the country. The parents were nominated by National-State-Teachers-of-the-Year because of how well these moms and dads raised their children. Looking back, the following traits were common tools they used during their parenting years:

1. Perseverance: For parents who forged ahead regardless of what others said or thought.
2. Compassion: For parents who chose to demonstrate consideration and sensitivity.
3. Diligence: For parents who demanded a strong work ethic.
4. Conviction: For parents who communicated what the family stood for, and against.
5. Creativity: For parents who needed to prioritize what was important in life.
6. Resiliency: For parents during physical, financial, or personal hardship.
7. Clarity: For parents who chose to leave little doubt what "NO" meant.
8. Vigilance: For parents who knew they were responsible for raising their children.
9. Accountability: For parents who taught their children consequences.
10. Forbearance: For parents who recognized that "delayed gratification" was good.
11. Discernment: For parents who taught their children right from wrong, good from evil.
12. Grace: For parents who understood what to ask God for.

If you look at the list, one could argue that these traits have little to do with "happiness." In fact, words like, "conviction," "compassion," and "forbearance," may be unpopular in a world where "courage," "forgiveness," and "self-sacrifice," are the exception, not the rule. Furthermore, I never heard one good parent draw a parallel between their quest for personal happiness and raising children. For them, they simply had a job to do.

Maybe they were too busy spending time with their children to worry about what they would get out of their investment. Perhaps they saw their job as a "calling" that demanded that they give their very best, regardless of dollars, time, or freedom lost. Ultimately parents who choose the needs of their children over their personal wants and desires have taken the "higher" road.

During the parenting project, I received a letter from a young man named Michael, who wrote about the gift his parents gave him and his brothers. In his correspondence he was responding to the following question: If "10" is indeed perfect, what number would he give his parents? His tribute says it all. *"If '10' is perfect I would have to give Mom and Dad about an '8.' They were not perfect. A lot of times when the perfect thing to do would have been to say, 'No we can't afford it,' they would say, 'We'll see if there isn't someway we can work it out.' There were times when they really had work to do and they took the time to play with me. They were not perfect, but then perfect people do not need love. It is their imperfections that make them special, that make them my parents. They are close enough to perfect for me."*

For Michael, and tens of thousands of other sons and daughters, parental perfection will never be measured by how much "quality" time they received from their moms and dads. Rather, it will be measured by love and sacrifice. And that's why eternal happiness awaits those imperfect parents whose "8" will be good enough for God.

A final memory is in order. The parents involved in the interview project all had varying degrees of challenges. There were single parents whose time, not to mention energy, was often tapped. There were families where one or more of the children were handicapped. Unemployment, poor health, rebellious teens, and day-to-day temptations were commonplace. But in the end, almost every parent agreed that there were five reasons why they were successful at raising children: Faith in God, discipline, demanding the best from their kids, open communication, and time. Without the latter, all else fails.

Something to Ponder

Do you recall the times in your life when a parent, friend, teacher, coach, neighbor, or work associate informed you that they didn't have time to respond to your needs? How did you feel about their decision? I've been there. When George, a mildly retarded teenager, was told by the boys on my team that we didn't have the time to teach him the game of baseball, I was ashamed that I didn't have the courage to stand up for him. On another occasion, after coming home from work one day Cindy politely led me to the kitchen window where I could observe my son Robbie (then our only child) peeking through the picket fence watching the neighbor's two little boys playing together. Prior to that moment, I wasn't sure if I had the time to be a Dad for more than one child. Andrew was born nine months later.

We all have the potential to add agendas to our life. We can find time to entertain others. We can take on extra job responsibilities. We can watch more television, attend more sporting events, or participate in shopping excursions. What we can't do is add "time" to our twenty-four-hour day. Given this scientific restriction, are you spending the time you have, doing the best you can, for those you love? Have you figured out the correct formula to balance family, work, and community responsibilities? Are you prepared to stand before almighty God and answer the question: "How did you use the time I gave you?"

And if this same God informed you that you only had one week to live, what would you do with that gift? Would you run to your TV guide to make sure that you wouldn't miss any good movies, sporting events, soap operas, talk shows, or reality programs? Would you block out your schedule to meet with your financial advisor or attorney? Would you arrange that last round of golf, throw a party for your friends, or take that promised vacation? And if you did these things would you be happy?

Or would you do something else? Would time with family surface as your new number one priority? Do you think you could find the heart to write a letter to that estranged friend? Is there someone or some organization whose plea for help might suddenly be heard? And what is the chance that you would take the time to pray, asking God for mercy for all you've done or failed to do? What other things might occupy your final one hundred sixty-eight hours?

If you have trouble imagining how you would spend that final week, put yourself in the mindset of the prisoner on death row, the lonely grandparent with no family visitors, the child with no parent to play with, or the spouse with no one to love. For them and tens of thousands like them, the issue is not, and never will be, quality time.

Your choice is simple: In your pursuit of happiness, be sure that your playbook includes "spiritual" time management. Those that do are less likely to be caught napping. *"For you know neither the day nor the hour"* (Mt 25: 13).

CHOICE #4
FIDELITY or BETRAYAL

"Eureka"

The bowling scoreboard identified the pretty blond as Cindy. With that knowledge and a little courage, I got the nerve up to ask where she lived. "I can't see boys," was her answer. Undeterred, I tried another approach. "What's your last name?" Again, her response was the same. "I understand," I said, "I was just curious." Recognizing my intentions, Cindy coyly said, "Detroit." "Huh?" "Detroit, that's where I live," she teased. My future search had just been narrowed down to a city of 4 million people.

I lived in Hazel Park, a suburb north of the automotive city. I figured that with some gentle persuasion, more detailed information might be forthcoming. I made a third attempt. "What part of Detroit?" I asked. With a half smile she said, "Well, I live on a street, near a street, named Eureka." With this new intelligence I figured I better not push my luck.

The following day, July 9, 1964, at approximately one in the afternoon, my friend Randy stopped over. I immediately tried to convince him to help me find the blue-eyed blond I had met the day before. "Let me see if I've got this right," he said. "You met this girl named Cindy, who wouldn't give you her last name, phone number, or address, other than the fact that she lives 'on a street, near a street, named Eureka.'" "You got it," I responded. "Furthermore," Randy continued, "according to your map, Eureka runs six miles!" "Correct," I confirmed. "Are you nuts?" he demanded. "C'mon Randy, we've got nothing to do anyways. Let's just walk in to Detroit and see if we kind find her." I added, "Besides, you never know where Divine Providence might lead us." After five minutes of debate, Randy finally agreed to join in the search for a girl that, as he said, "may not even be home, wherever that is."

We followed the map toward the mythical land of "Eureka." Running out of conversation, Randy finally stopped. "Look David," he began, "we have been walking for over an hour in ninety-degree heat and we still don't know if we have another mile or SIX miles to go." His logic was hard to refute. "I'm heading back home," he announced. "Randy, we can't stop now. Eureka is the next street." "True," came the terse reply, "however, you do recall that she said she doesn't live on Eureka, but on some block either side of Eureka!" "All right Randy, you're right, this was foolish." We turned for home heading down a street named Justine. As we walked in silence, I noticed a little girl about age six riding her bike towards us. For some strange reason I flagged her down. "By any chance, do you know of any girl named Cindy that lives around here?" I inquired. Without hesitating, the little girl pointed to the house we were standing in front of and said, "Cindy lives right there." She was in the backyard with her sister Nancy. It was her birthday. And we have been married thirty-six years! Postscript: *Eureka*, is the Greek word for, "I have found!" For a sixteen-year-old boy it spelled H-A-P-P-I-N-E-S-S.

For the next three years we dated steadily. Then one summer night in August after returning from the popular movie *To Sir With Love*, it was time to say goodbye. "Cindy," I began, "tomorrow I am leaving for military service which will most likely lead to at least one tour in Vietnam." Holding back my tears I continued. "A month from now you will be entering college where you will likely meet one or more guys that will ask you out." The thought was painful. "You need to get on with your life," I said. Walking her up to the door I stopped and kissed her goodnight for what I thought would be the last time. "Cindy, I will always love you. Good luck. Goodbye." I turned and walked slowly back to my car. It was the unhappiest moment of my life.

But it would not be the last time. During the next three years of active duty I received a letter from her EVERY DAY! This long distance love affair eventually led to the altar. On May 22, 1970, we were married at a Catholic church in Warren, Michigan. The words, *for better or worse, for richer or poorer, in sickness and in health*, seemed an easy proposition. After all, didn't people get married because they wanted to be happy for the rest of their lives? It was so logical.

Unfortunately, "happiness" is too often short-lived as other distractions vie for our attention. I had to complete my education. I had to work full time. I had to play ball on weekends with my friends. I had to be happy. But something happened during my hedonistic journey.

I had just received a promotion at General Motors in the Fisher Body Division. It was my first day in my new assignment. Early afternoon I felt a slight twinge of discomfort on my left side. As the workday ended I headed off to class. That evening the pain increased. By the time class ended I was nearly bent over in agony. Somehow I managed to drive home. Cindy took one look at me and said, "David, you don't look well." She gave me some aspirin and tucked me in bed.

The following morning all "hell" broke loose. I was in severe pain and had projectile vomiting. My wife rushed me to the hospital and for the next five days I had every test known to modern medicine to determine why I was so sick and had a swollen abdomen. As I waited for lab results, I kept thinking about my job, my classes, and my softball season. Cindy had other things on her mind as there was the distinct possibility that her husband of three years was dying of cancer! There was a serious disconnect, and I was the reason for the malfunction.

On the sixth day, a surgeon came into my room. "David," he began, "I've got to be honest with you. We don't know why you are so sick. But what we do know is you now have poison in your blood stream." I lay there in silence waiting for my death sentence. Cindy was crying. The doctor continued. "Monday morning we're going to open you up and see what's causing your illness." With that, he left the room.

When you are twenty-five years old lying in a hospital bed with your young wife weeping at your side, you suddenly realize what is important in life. Class assignments didn't matter anymore. The loss of an entire semester was irrelevant. My new job would have to wait. And as for my team, well most of the guys had already written me off for the season. All that was left was all that was important: Cindy.

"Gangrene? But how? Why?" I demanded to know. "Frankly, David, no one on the medical staff has a clue," came the doctor's response. "All I can say is that you're a lucky young man because your wife brought you in when she did, and now that same lady is ready to nurse you back to health." His words stung my soul. The Cindy I had no time for had been at my side for seven straight days. My wife was honoring her marriage vows. The question was whether or not I would keep my end of the bargain.

"Eureka" had struck again. Only this time, my search for happiness would only be fulfilled by making another happy. In my "heart of hearts," I believe the good Lord sent me a physical cross to carry at a time in my life when I was close to jeopardizing what it meant to love and be loved. My fidelity to my marriage took on a new significance. And more important, my personal promise to God to "love and cherish" my wife would become a life-long call-to-action.

In the Old Testament's Book of Sirach, the author gently reminds the reader that *"A good wife is a generous gift bestowed upon him, who fears the Lord; Be he rich or poor, his heart is content, and a smile is ever on his face"* (Sir 26: 3–4). I have been smiling ever since.

A Message for My Sons

When my son Robbie was engaged I took the time to write him a personal letter to be delivered just days before his marriage to Kate. I wanted to share whatever wisdom I could, with the hope that my words might better prepare him for the life-long commitment he was about to make. Two years later I wrote a similar letter to his brother, Andrew, just before he walked down the aisle with his fiancée, Julie. Both versions were void of any reference to "happiness." The following excerpts put everything in perspective.

On "I Do"

"For better or worse, for richer or poorer, in sickness and in health, till death do you part," is your personal guarantee that you are willing to stick it out in good times and bad. It is an everlasting reminder that you intend to love her always even when she gives you reason not to. It means that today's love will be there tomorrow regardless of consequences. It demands that you have the courage to forgive and the humility to know when you need forgiveness. Most of all, it is your private tapestry that publicly displays how truthful you were to your marriage vows.

On "Children"

Should both of you be blessed with children be prepared for the sacrifices you are asked to make. Remember that there is no greater gift you can give than your time. Teach them discipline, lest someone else does. Teach them to discern right from wrong, good from evil, avoiding others who prefer "value-neutral" behaviors. Teach them a strong work ethic, and you and your wife will bask in the pride of their accomplishments. Teach them compassion and you will have kind grandchildren. Give them the gift of fidelity as evidenced by the love their parents have for each other. Teach them how to forgive and you will experience how quickly they forget their parents' mistakes. Be prepared to pay your parenting dues. The ROI is fantastic.

On "Love"

It is one thing to love a person for her beauty, quite another to love her at her worst. Loving one's sense of humor is no challenge. Tolerating one's moods is. Remembering birthdays, Christmas Day, and Valentine's Day comes naturally. Reminding her daily that you love her is a special talent. Deliver the "unexpected," and the chances of taking each other for granted are significantly reduced. Be kind. Be honest. Be compassionate. Most of all, forgive, lest you not be forgiven.

On "Temptation"

It will happen. The grass will look greener on the other side. The game will seem more important. The promotion will promise everything *you've* wanted. Sooner or later both of you will be tempted to put your own desires ahead of the vows you made to each other. Be on guard. You fell in love for a reason. Never forget why.

On "Success"

So how will you know if you are successful in life? It won't be measured by the size of your bank account, the car you drive, the title you hold, or the address on your mailbox. Rather, your personal portfolio will be measured by how you raised your children, how you loved and honored your spouse, how you shared your blessings with others, and what they say about you after you are gone.

On "God"

As the billboard states: "Enjoyed the wedding. Now invite me to the marriage." Don't wait for the hour of despair to cry out to God to save your marriage, your children or your soul. Engage Him who has given you each other. Ask the Holy Spirit to help you make the right decisions for the right reasons. Pray for the mercy of Christ for all you have done and will fail to do. And remember Mary, the Mother of all God's children. As you love your children, so does she love their parents.

I believe that if new husbands focused on the above themes, there would be less sadness in the world. A similar invitation will be extended to my daughter, Kelly, who will soon be joined in Holy Matrimony to a fine young man named Massi.

A Message for My Mother

Many years ago I came across a personal help column that reprinted a very special letter reminding the newspaper's readership that we must never abandon those who never abandoned us. The following was written by an anonymous person in Florida.

"Yesterday was an old man's birthday. He was 91. He awakened earlier than usual, bathed, shaved and put on his best clothes. Surely they would come today, he thought.

"He didn't take his daily walk to the gas station to visit with the old-timers of the community because he wanted to be right there when they came.

"He sat on the front porch with a clear view of the road so he could see them coming. Surely they would come today.

"He decided to skip his noon nap because he wanted to be up when they came.

"He has six children. Two of his daughters and their married children live within four miles. They hadn't been to see him for such a long time. But today was his birthday. Surely they would come today.

"At suppertime he refused to cut the cake and asked that the ice cream be left in the freezer. He wanted to wait and have dessert with them when they came.

"About 9 o'clock he went to his room and got ready for bed. His last words before turning out the lights were, 'Promise to wake me up when they come.'

"It was his birthday and he was 91."

My mother will soon be ninety years old. She doesn't know her age. She's forgotten the names of her grandchildren. And more frequently, her only child is nothing more than a familiar face. My mother has Alzheimer's disease. Cindy's parents both died of cancer. My wife was at their side for several weeks waiting for God to take her mom and dad. We both understand that "fidelity" to the family includes caring for those who cared for us. And though neither of us wishes to be a burden to our children, we believe that they will be at our side when our time comes.

Betrayal

Unfortunately "fidelity" is too often replaced by "betrayal." A father refuses to play catch with his son because he wants to go play golf with his buddies. A mother "dumps" her child at a local daycare center so she can go shopping with her friends. Siblings resist visiting their parents in the senior citizen home because other things are more important. And a wife or husband laments the time they must sacrifice to "love" their spouse.

Sometimes "betrayal" exacts a greater price. A husband starves his wife to death so that he can go on with HIS life. A mother aborts her unborn child so that SHE can go on with her life. Parents abandon their handicapped children to society so THEY can go on with their lives.

Meanwhile, Hollywood movies endorse euthanasia positioning the hero's "right-to-die" as the only alternative; courts overrule parents who wish only to council their daughter before she terminates a life; politicians filibuster each other to death on issues that were once sacred; scientists actively defend their right to take creation out of the hands of the Creator; and physicians prescribe "numbing" drugs so the parents are not distracted by over-active kids.

These "quality-of-life" initiatives are disguised as recipes for happiness. But the artificial joys are short-lived as infidelity destroys a marriage; infanticide destroys a life; injustice destroys a community; and immorality destroys a nation.

Other betrayals occur beyond the family unit. Company loyalty is replaced with corporate greed and worker laziness. The *Ten Commandments* are selectively chosen to correspond with the needs and desires of today's "cafeteria Christians." And allegiance to our country's flag, wavers as both personal and political agendas serve to divide a nation. In the end, our search for happiness only leads to despair and hopelessness as fidelity to God, family, and nation are sacrificed on the altar of betrayal.

In Dante's *Divine Comedy* there are nine circles of Hell. Each circle represents greater and greater evil. Three characters in history share residency with Satan: Judas Iscariot, betrayer of Christ, Brutus, the Roman general and politician, and his co-conspirator, Cassius, both of whom conspired to assassinate Julius Caesar. These souls paid the price for their infidelity. If only they had learned from Mary Magdalene, who, with the Mother of God remained at the foot of the cross until the very end. The disciple John could have also taught them a thing or two as he was the only apostle of Jesus who did not run away.

There have been many role models throughout history. One of my favorites was Helen Keller who was quoted as saying, *"Many persons have a wrong idea of what constitutes true happiness. It is not attained through self-gratification but through fidelity to a worthy* purpose." And that "purpose," I believe, has nothing to do with personal happiness in this life, but everything to do with eternal happiness in the next.

Something to Ponder

When I was in first grade, I remember receiving a "cameo" part in the school Christmas pageant. I was playing the role of a Jewish man who was one of the suitors lined up to ask Mary for her hand in holy matrimony. When asked what was the most important trait I looked for in a wife, my three-word script was, "I, her loyalty." Apparently my response wasn't good enough because someone named Joseph won the day. Nevertheless, loyalty, like fidelity, has become synonymous with faithfulness. And who among us would not want to surround ourselves with individuals we can trust?

All of us know cases where infidelity led to the destruction of a marriage and often times a family. With so much bad publicity on the impact of divorce, one must ask why so many couples abandon their wedding vows? What happened to their dream to "live happily ever after?" And how many "soul-mate" searchers end up in a worse relationship than they had before they decided to walk away? Do you believe that society's "no-fault divorce" mentality is compatible with the pursuit of happiness? Having recently attended a wedding where the groom had three children from two different women, most family members were on their second or third marriage, and the preacher assigned to preside over the ceremony received his credentials on-line, I couldn't help but wonder what the chances were that the bride and groom will remain faithful to one another.

Fidelity is not reserved for the marriage bed. Why do you suppose there are so many unhappy corporate executives who frequently abandon the company that gave them the opportunity to excel? Can you explain the thinking behind the multi-million dollar athlete who, after winning the championship, sells his services to the highest bidder? And how do you feel about those "citizens" who condemn the nation's leadership for reducing their freedoms in public arenas, and then turn around and criticize the same government for not protecting them during terrorist attacks? Can you identify other scenarios? What about dissension between church authorities, labor unions, educators, law and order, political parties, neighborhoods, athletic departments, and others. The list is endless.

Ask yourself three questions. First, if the original intent of "warring" parties was to build something that would make both happy, then why are so many in our society so willing to abandon their dream? Second, if the decision to walk away only leads to unhappiness, what makes them think that the next engagement will be different? And third, how many unfaithful souls do you think will be happy in their next life?

Perhaps this last question justifies the thinking of St. Francis de Sales, who wrote, "*They who wish to live happily and in perfect fidelity, must accustom themselves to live according to reason, rule and obedience, not according to their own inclinations.*" Maybe Abraham Lincoln's take on the problem is even simpler. The sixteenth president of the United States was once quoted as saying, "*People are just as happy as they make up their minds to be.*" In either case, another choice must be made: Fidelity or betrayal.

CHOICE #5
CONVICTION or COMPLACENCY

Hell's Gate

Returning to Dante's *Divine Comedy,* we find the poet in a "dark wood" staring at a rod iron gate with a sign that reads, "Abandon every hope, all you who enter." Dante enters through the gate and begins his journey down to the nine circles of Hell. In the first circle he encounters nameless souls whose sin had been *complacency* as they chose to make no choice, defend no cause, or demonstrate a total lack of concern. Clearly the local residents in this God-forsaken place are not happy. In retrospect, their decision "to sit on the fence" was too high a price to pay. Had they the courage and conviction to take a stand on one or more issues, things might have been different.

Ask anyone over fifty years of age and they will probably tell you that today's world is filled with complacent individuals who hide behind "politically correct" labels. These "fence sitters" rally behind a new vocabulary offering phrases and terms like "values clarification," "situational ethics," "moral relativism," "victimology," and "entitlements." Their "freedom follies" lead to distorted decisions directly opposed to the Constitution or Ten Commandments.

For a nation that encourages "the pursuit of happiness," there are increasing signs that all is not well in this land of opportunity. Too many children experience poor nutrition or have no health insurance. And though our medical technology is the envy of the world, America still has a disappointing infant mortality rate.

In education, increasing illiteracy, dropouts, low test scores, unqualified teachers, poor materials, poor schools, not to mention sinking morale, are common headlines featured in newspapers around the country. Worse yet, many of today's college graduates offer weak resumes because of inadequate writing skills, questionable work experience, and little or no community service. Further, many tenured professors are often indifferent when it comes to going the extra mile for their students. In one example, the Dean of the Journalism Department from a well-known "big ten" college was contacted to see if she could recommend some upcoming graduates that qualified for an entry-level, high-profile communications position. After waiting six weeks for a response, the employer decided to contact a competitive university to see if there were any candidates on their campus that needed a JOB! That same day three students were recommended by the chair of that school's Journalism Department. Unknowingly, qualified students at the big ten school lost an opportunity to interview because of a complacent faculty member who took little or no interest in their future.

On the family front, divorce, domestic violence, child abuse/neglect, and infidelity take their toll on this sacred institution. Challenges mount as parental involvement continues to decline. That's why many of today's parents and their children are drowning in a sea of stress. Who will listen to their S.O.S.?

Other societal diseases include poverty with its homelessness and unemployment cycles; gang violence; skyrocketing absenteeism, sub-standard quality and service, and low productivity in the workplace; racial discrimination; alcohol, drug, smoking, and gambling addictions; and a menu of pornographic temptations courtesy of television programming, radio talk shows, magazine features, movies, music, video games, concerts, and the Internet.

Maybe the reason why there is so much discontent in this world is the ninth letter of the alphabet. If *I* am too caught up in my own world, the needs and concerns of others become insignificant. If *I* run the risk of upsetting my personal contentment by getting involved, the courage needed to make a difference in my community will suffer. And if *I* choose to walk away, the role model my family, friends, neighbors, and colleagues so desperately need will fail to materialize.

Ironically, the letter "I" is often a recipe for unhappiness. Consider these ingredients: Injustice, Immorality, Infanticide, Infidelity, Idleness, Intolerance, Illicitness, Indifference, Inhumanity, Iniquity, Insufferableness, and Invidiousness. Added to this list is "Ideology," which sums up who we are and what we believe. And it is this personal blueprint that will ultimately determine whether we walk through the gate of Heaven or Hell.

The Pilate Conspiracy

"What is truth?" Pilate asked Jesus. The answer to that simple question is not so simple. Ask a reporter and the "we'll report, you decide" response will be forthcoming. Watch attorneys defend conflicting interpretations of the law. Call a physician for a second opinion, and you may need a third. Challenge a politician about his or her personal attacks against an opponent, and you will hear the "public has a right to know" speech. Inquire why a member of the clergy broke his vow of obedience, and you may hear a sermon on why the Church is wrong. Audit business executive company balance sheets, and you may be asked to testify. Interrogate union leadership about their misrepresentation of the facts, and you could cross the picket line. If you capitulate to teachers' demands for higher wages, without the right to measure student performance, you will reap what you have sown. Attempting to differentiate between a Hollywood entertainer's public and private image is like trying to convince the paparazzi to make an appointment. And complaining about the money professional athletes earn after you buy tickets to see them compete is at best hypocritical.

Why all the confusion? What's so difficult about standing up for what you believe in? And how on earth can members of a complacent society continue their search for happiness, when their inaction leads to so much despair? I believe there are four barriers standing in the way of courage and conviction.

Barrier I—In Search of Sin

Our search must begin with a clear position. Evil exists. Sin exists. Satan exists. These truths necessitate a return to the Ten Commandments from which discussions about morals, values, and ethics emanate. Author James Michener may have said it best: "*Values are the emotional rules by which a nation governs itself. Values summarize folk wisdom by which a society disciplines itself. And values are reminders that individuals obey to bring order and meaning into their lives.*" He concludes, "*Without values, nations, societies, and individuals can pitch straight to Hell.*" In short, we must avoid the sickness of sin and death of the soul.

To defend this position demands a certain conviction necessary to bury an avalanche of excuses for not taking a stand. If you agree that each moral situation has its own set of circumstances, then you must also accept the possibility that an offense against you may be justified. If you argue that no one has a right to force their morality on you, then you must also accept others' interpretations of right and wrong. If you accept the argument that it is a "sin" to be judgmental, then you must avoid criticizing others for their decisions regardless of the consequences. If you are convinced that a person who commits a crime is the real victim because he or she had a rough upbringing, then you must explain why thousands of others in similar neighborhoods made right choices. And if you are willing to trade in your personal safety and the well-being of your family for "civil liberties," then I suggest you heed author George Orwell's suggestion that, "*There are some ideas so preposterous that only an intellectual could believe them.*"

History has proved that there is evil in the world. The Marquis de Sade, a French noble and atheist, had a simple philosophy: There is no God. There is no Hell. There is no soul.

But when a husband murders his wife and her unborn child, when a father stabs his nine-year-old daughter to death, or when a mother drowns her two young boys, one has to wonder what drives such horrors. If college students argue that the Holocaust was nothing more than one man's solution to a problem or that human sacrifice in certain societies should be permissible, we must question what's behind such madness.

When a U.S. Senator argues that his only crime for fondling women was misjudgment of their character, or a company CEO states that it wasn't his fault that he stole 1 million dollars, something is terribly wrong in our society. And if a college professor tries to convince his students that rape may be wrong only because their ancestors agreed, an author argues that the breakdown of the family is a good thing, or a national organization is allowed to promote pedophilia to its membership, "no-fault" soul insurance is here to stay. Clearly, our nation has lost its moral compass.

One "truth" can't be denied: avoiding controversy allows evil to fester. In a desperate attempt to find happiness, too many self-indulgent individuals will not get involved with anything that could jeopardize their comfort zone. If they choose not to define sin, believe in Hell, or defend truth, they run the risk of trading centuries old morality for twenty-first-century immorality. What was once obvious is dangerously becoming inconsequential. And when good is substituted for evil because it temporarily protects their self-interests, they only delay the inevitable: death.

On one hand we "preach" the importance of good character; on the other hand we endorse bad characters. When a President of the United States sits in office during good economic times, should we look the other way when his immoral behavior becomes an embarrassment to the nation? When a CEO increases the company's portfolio, does his performance excuse the board from challenging business decisions that are unethical? When a celebrity's indiscretions go public, should not the public abandon their idolatry?

Some years ago a Brinks truck flipped over spilling out cash, coins, and valuable stamps. Both drivers were injured in the accident. Passing motorists and residents stopped to grab what they could before the police arrived. Over $550,000 was stolen. Less than $25 was returned. If evil doesn't exist and sin is nothing more than human compulsions, then worldly happiness at the expense of others will become the rule of law. But if evil does exist and sin is the ticket to Hell, then we would all do well to heed the warning of Russian author Alexander Solzhenitsyn, who said, "*The line between good and evil runs right down the middle of every human heart.*"

Those who "sit on the fence" run the risk of landing on the wrong side of good. And when that happens, all hope for eternal happiness is vanquished. But if we find the courage to stand up for what is right, the day will come when someone who is right will stand up for us.

Barrier II—Compassion Versus Compassion

Again we must have the courage to state our position clearly. For purposes of addressing this barrier, a single "truth" must be acknowledged: the sanctity of life represents a full and complete recognition that all human life, from conception to death, is sacred. By definition capital punishment, euthanasia, and abortion are morally wrong. Said another way, God gave us life. He did not give us permission to destroy that life!

You have all heard the arguments. Doesn't life begin at birth? Is it not a woman's right to do with her body what she wants? What if she is raped? Is it right to bring a deformed baby into this world? If cloning can deliver a more "perfect" child, isn't this scientific progress? What's the difference between capital punishment and justice? What right do we have to tell people who are suffering in pain that they have no authority to take their life?

The Fifth Commandment, "*Thou Shall Not Kill*," is where the debate ends. If you accept this teaching, then there is no room for fence sitting. When a woman goes to her doctor to get an abortion, the unborn child inside her womb is referred to as a "fetus." But if another woman goes to the same doctor and he knows she wants to have the child, "baby" is the ordained title. When you hear politicians nervously defend their pro-abortion position as "the right to choose" with a caveat that they themselves would never indulge in such behavior, you are listening to the height of hypocrisy. When a judge overturns a parent's right to learn about their daughter's pending abortion, but allows the same mother and father to block school nurses from giving their child an aspirin, you are witnessing an abomination.

As society continues to tolerate right-to-die initiatives, more and more of the helpless in our culture will become victims. Children in the womb with a less than perfect mind or body are candidates for extinction. If Dad is unemployed or

Mom is considered too old to raise another child, the abortion advocates are ready to sell their solution. If a teenage daughter is comatose or a grandfather is in pain, Hemlock Society membership will demand to know why these "victims" should be kept alive?

In the embryo supermarket of the future, "designer" clones will be purchased from a mail order catalogue. And should your teenage daughter wait long enough before her abortion, she may fetch premium fees as fetal-part brokers give new meaning to "body part" shops. Bizarre? Don't kid yourself. Adolph Hitler's quest for a superior race led to the extermination of millions of undesirables. As this tragedy was going on, "fatherland" residents, who knew about the horrors of Auschwitz, were guilty of tolerance. And if our nation's complacency continues, we will fulfill political philosopher William Burke's prediction: *"This country is plunging headlong into a science-fiction nightmare; in the final analysis, fetal tissue implants are not that much different from Nazi lampshades made of Jewish skin. Both intend to put by-products of murder to good use."*

Complacency is easy. You can look the other way while millions of children are slaughtered in the womb. You can vote with your pocketbook ignoring the agenda of "choice" candidates whose political platform is license to end the lives of others. You can disregard scientific breakthroughs announcing yet another step toward a "perfect" man-made human being. You can hide behind "compassion" rhetoric that twists the literal meaning of the word—to suffer with—to no suffering. You can do all these things. But in the end God is still in control. And He expects you to defend the sanctity of life regardless of consequences to you or those at the center of the debate. If you find this conviction hard to accept, then you might want to reflect on the anonymous quotation below:

> *"When God wants an important thing done in this world or a wrong righted, He goes about it in a singular way. He doesn't release thunderbolts, or stir up earthquakes. God simply has a tiny baby born, perhaps of a very humble home, perhaps of a very humble mother. And God puts the idea or purpose into the mother's heart. And she puts it in the baby's mind and then—God waits. The great events of this world are not battles and elections and earthquakes or thunderbolts. The great events are babies, for each child comes with the message that God is not yet discouraged with humanity, but is still expecting goodwill to become incarnate in each human life."*

Make no mistake, the God that gave you life is the same God that expects you to defend life. And if this philosophy makes you uneasy, ask yourself these questions. How many women who have had abortions do you know that are truly "happy" with their choice? Do you know any person who, after pulling the plug on their loved one, goes around telling their friends and family how "happy" they are with their decision? Does "death row" media coverage bring you great joy?

What is it that is so unsettling about these issues? Could it be that in the inner depths of our God-given conscience we know that there is something evil about killing members of the human family? Conversely, why do we find ourselves drawn to the smiles of handicapped children? Why do we comment that parents who raise such kids are "special?" And what is it about children of seriously ill parents who refuse to give up hope. Why do they inspire us? Maybe the answer lies in the knowledge that the sacrifice that they are asked to give begins and ends with love. As for the rest of us, we would do well to worry less about our personal happiness and more about the happiness of others.

Barrier III—In Search of Symbiosis

The third barrier to "truth" is the tiresome debate over the separation of church and state. Was not this country founded by a religious people whose constitution was based on Judeo-Christian morality? Why then would a nation's best political and legal minds quarantine God from His people? Why should the demands of a few dictate how and when we celebrate Christmas or Hanukkah? Why is a national youth organization with over one hundred years of history continuously challenged because parents of one child are offended by a single word—God? Why in troubling times do politicians invoke the name of God, then turn their back on Him when judges forbid public schools from mentioning the Creator? Your conviction on such matters must be clear: separation of church and state does *NOT* mean separation from God!

This raging controversy has generated one ridiculous case after another. Football players can't pray before a high school game because someone might be offended. Prisoners are prohibited from having a Rosary because the symbol may represent gang affiliations. "Winter Holidays" have replaced the Christmas season. A ten-year-old public school child is prohibited from "crossing herself" during a moment of silence. Another little girl is banned from the school play because she wants to sing a Christmas carol. Her parents are told that the words may be offensive because they refer to the birth of Christ. Meanwhile there is a political movement to remove the words "under God" from the Pledge of Allegiance while "separation" proponents argue that Judeo-Christian teachings are undemocratic, insensitive, and judgmental.

Enough is enough! What will it take before parents have the courage to demand that CHRISTMAS plays are part of the CHRISTMAS season? How many sales must be rung up before the sales clerk has the guts to say, "Merry Christmas? Is there a public school coach out there who is willing to expose the team to a moment of prayer asking God to protect his players from injury? Will the school's administration back him up? Are there any CEO's reading these words that are willing to publicly support faith based youth organizations? And what about the millions of newspaper subscribers who privately complain about church and state separation debates, but never bother to write the editor, attend a town or school meeting, or call their state representative?

How can we be happy when every fabric of our society is unraveling? When will we recognize that "church and state" complacency is one of the main reasons why there is so much unhappiness? We need God in our lives. We need God in the affairs of our country. We need God in our families and our communities. But if we continue to hide behind First Amendment distortions, then we will ultimately have to answer to the ONE who said: *I tell you, everyone who acknowledges me before others the Son of Man will acknowledge before the angels of God. But whoever denies me before others will be denied before the angels of God* (Lk 12: 8–9).

<u>Barrier IV—Forbidden Fruit</u>

I would like to begin this discussion with an old proverb: "No snowflake in an avalanche ever feels responsible." When we bury our society in an avalanche of freedoms, we quickly discover that "freedom" without "responsibility" has its consequences. Arguments for sexual liberation, free speech, and freedom of choice lead to greater sins of infidelity, vulgarity, and abortion, to name a few.

Proponents of unlimited freedoms will challenge those who believe in common decency. The following barrage of self-serving questions sets the table with bad fruit. Since divorce is so common, why not consider each relationship as a life-stage allowing men and women to search for their "soul mate?" Isn't sexual experimentation justified because "everyone is doing it"? Besides, who really gets hurt if one's spouse never finds out about the occasional one-night stand? And how do you explain the popularity of pornography?

Other freedom demands are cloaked behind the "magical" word censorship. If you don't want to be exposed to indecent material on radio, television, or the Internet, just turn the dial or don't dial up, is the recommendation. And some of these "freedom fighters" will go so far as to challenge parents who dare to censor their children from the world-wide web, charging that such adult behavior only teaches the youngest generation "intolerance." The absurdity of their position is magnified in "tolerance" for several organizations like the *North American Man/Boy Love Association* that advocates sex with children; government-funded sex education groups that encourage schools to teach reproductive biology, abortion, masturbation, and homosexuality to children as young as five years of age; and public libraries that demand the right to loan out any material to any child regardless of content. These defenders of "rights" argue that censorship is *not* what this country was founded upon. Their rationale is that freedom of speech and expression is far more important than what is seen, said, or heard. Benjamin Hooks, past Executive Director of the NAACP disagrees. "*The whole philosophy of our country has changed to accept immorality, degeneracy, pornographic movies.*" Mr. Hooks goes on. "*I'm the world's greatest advocate of the First Amendment, but somehow we've got to have freedom with responsibility.*" More direct are the comments Senator Robert Bryd made while speaking on the Senate floor: "*If we in this nation continue to sow the images of murder, violence, drug abuse, sadism, arrogance, irreverence, blasphemy, perversion, pornography, and aberration before the eyes of millions of children, year after year and day after day, we should not be surprised if the foundations of our society rot away as if from leprosy.*"

Poppies?

In the 1939 movie *The Wizard of Oz*, there is a scene where the evil witch is looking through a crystal ball observing Dorothy, the Lion, Scarecrow, and Tin Man, walking through a field of poppies. "Sleep" is the adversary's invitation to the heroine and her three friends. In another story, the biblical character Samson was asleep when Delilah cut his hair, draining him of his strength. And one of the reasons why Adolph Hitler lost the war was because he was sound asleep during the D-Day invasion on June 6, 1944.

Is society drugged by some sort of modern day poppy that results in a complacent mindset that destroys families, communities, and nations? Why do we allow television commentators to suffocate the airwaves with their nightly updates on the sordid details of the latest celebrity scandal? How is it that so many parents live in fear for their children's safety but do little to take the necessary steps to eradicate evil in their homes? Why do politicians tolerate unacceptable behavior among their colleagues at a time when the moral character of our nation and its people continues to decline? What defense can Hollywood directors produce for making movies that glorify gratuitous sex, extreme violence, vulgar language, abortion, euthanasia, and other anti-Christian themes? Shouldn't private and public companies that profit from video, cable, and website sales of similar trash be held accountable? Speaking of accountability, when will college professors be disciplined by the school's administration for promoting personal ideology in the classroom? And what will it take before judges have the courage to defend God and His laws?

Because we lack conviction there is growing unhappiness in the world. Almost every week there is a new story on the latest family slaughter by a deranged relative; the abduction of another child; pregnancy, abortion, and disease trends; teen obesity rates; violence in schools; addiction epidemics; immoral fads; and divorce, depression, and unemployment statistics.

In one church the following support group meetings were posted in the bulletin:

> Sunday 2:00 p.m.—Cocaine anonymous
> Monday 3:00 p.m.—Survivors of incest
> Monday 5:00 p.m.—Debtors anonymous
> Tuesday 7:00 p.m.—Alcoholics anonymous
> Wednesday 6:30 p.m.—Sex addicts anonymous
> Wednesday 8:30 p.m.—Overeaters anonymous
> Thursday 6:00 p.m.—Self-abusers anonymous
> Thursday 8:00 p.m.—Victims of divorce
> Friday 7:00 p.m.—Co-dependents of sex addicts

This church is not unique. Nor are the tens of thousands of school administrators that must budget a significant portion of their operating funds to help students avoid self-destruction. Corporate America, government agencies, hospitals, and other non-profit organizations also pay the price to help workers cope with their personal problems.

The road to happiness is filled with social landmines capable of destroying the dreams and aspirations travelers have for themselves and those they love. We must all be educated on the issues, take a stand for what's right, and believe in our calling.

Two individuals I have the honor of knowing have done just that. Their journey is a remarkable testimony of what can happen when one person has both the conviction and courage to follow their heart.

The Story of Tat

When she was a little toddler growing up in Minnesota, this child would go around the house babbling, "Tat, Tat, Tat, Tat…" That was how Tat got her name. When I met this charming eighty-four-year-old, I learned what it meant to have a high energy level. Equally impressive was the fact that she still rode her bike to daily Mass. It was her oldest son, Robert, who insisted in introducing me to his mom. And what a "mother" she is. She has eight children, twenty-eight grandchildren, and seventeen great-grandchildren. But the fact that she has been blessed by such a wonderful family is not what got my attention.

What sets Tat apart is conviction. After her husband had experienced his seventh heart attack, dying at age fifty-one, Tat decided that she had no time to be a widow. There was work to be done. So after burying the love of her life, Tat joined the pro-life movement and proceeded to set up forty-two right-to-life chapters throughout the state of Michigan. She almost went broke paying the long distance phone bills needed to open each new pregnancy center.

Tat was so successful that she was asked to join the Republican Party to help the governor's pro-life platform. Because of her reputation, she was invited to attend party meetings in the nation's capital no less than fifteen times. At one of those meetings the five-foot two-inch advocate was surrounded by a number of fellow politicians who demanded to know if the rumor was true that she recommended a Democratic candidate for a seat currently held by one of her party members. Her response: "You better believe it. There is no way I am going to help a pro-abortion butcher get elected to office!"

At age seventy-four Tat stepped down from her leadership position because her conscience would not allow her to accept a stipend for her role as a state board member. But again she found she had too much time on her hands.

Recognizing that the local Catholic school, where all eight of her children had attended, was in a financial bind, Tat helped start a foundation raising over 1.5 million dollars. One day the local bishop called to inform her that since the school was located in his diocese, he was confiscating the fund. "Not on my watch," was her response. To prove her point she engaged the help of a canon lawyer who eventually helped Tat win her case against local church authorities!

After mesmerizing me with her story for some two hours, Tat politely announced, "I would like to talk longer David, but I have an important meeting I have to attend." I understood.

There is an unusual footnote to Tat's story. For many years she has offered a number of special novenas to St. Theresa, better known as "The Little Flower."

When Theresa was but fifteen years of age, it was reported that during a papal visit Swiss guards had to physically remove the young teenager from the Vatican because she began to disagree with the Pope on when she would be allowed to enter the convent.

I couldn't help but notice the similarities between St. Theresa and Tat. In fact, Tat reminds me of another little lady who had the same demeanor. Mother Teresa of Calcutta, like Tat, was a defender of the unborn and an admirer of "The Little Flower." One day, both of these saints will be among the first to welcome Tat into God's kingdom.

The Orphan

At age eight John Shinsky was placed in an orphanage. At age twelve he was placed in a foster home. At age eighteen he was selected as an Academic All American in high school and eventually received the same honor when he graduated from Michigan State University four years later. When John was in his early thirties, he made a prediction: He was going to build a home for children. John's faith gave him the courage to state, "I don't know what kind of students the home will serve or even where it will be built. But I have a dream that someday this will be possible."

The first time I met John Shinsky was at a press conference announcing a program entitled, "I've Got Heart." The purpose of the program was to engage elementary students in a series of academic and service challenges that would earn them the opportunity to attend a professional baseball game and receive a special *I've Got Heart* shirt. The event was attended by the mayor, school administrators, and several community leaders from organizations that supported the initiative.

At the conclusion of the press conference, John came up to me and introduced himself. "David, my name is John Shinsky and I think this program is something Michigan State University should be involved in." I later learned that John was one of the top administrative officers serving the city's public school system. His six-foot four-inch football frame was impressive as was his confidence that a big ten university would show any kind of interest in a program targeted at elementary school children. "Mr. Shinsky," I countered, "I'm new here in Lansing and I'm afraid I don't know the right people to speak with at the university." John smiled and said, "I do." With that, he excused himself. Less than ten minutes later, Shinsky reappeared. "It's all set. Tomorrow you and I are meeting with Michigan State's Athletic Director." Three months later one of the largest colleges in the country would publicly endorse the "I've Got Heart" project.

At the time I first met John, he was responsible for the Lansing school system's special education division. In addition to his full-time position, John found time to chair multiple community charity events, conduct training sessions for future school administrators at seminars all over the country, and was a radio commentator during Michigan State Spartan games.

I found his commitment to the community and the children he served refreshing. Little did I know that even with all his personal and professional involvement, John had a more important agenda in the works. He was intent on building "The City of Children," a twelve-building orphanage located in Matamoros, Mexico. John's calling would fulfill the promise he made sixteen years earlier.

But how does one go about fulfilling a dream that calls for unbelievable time, talent, and treasure? For John Shinsky, it began with a conversation with a young man on an airplane who was working at an orphanage during spring break. This chance encounter resulted in John visiting a special home for poor children. His experience eventually led to a personal decision to get involved. Then he was introduced to two sisters, one ninety-two, the other, one hundred years of age. Together these young ladies have personally helped build over 1000 homes for the poor. Both of these women inspired John to move forward with his aspirations to build an orphanage for children. From there, John began placing calls to a few key friends. First there was the CEO of a busing company who agreed to provide the necessary transportation of labor and materials across the border. Then help came from a retired professional football player who was recently inducted into the Hall of Fame. This gentleman agreed to contact other ex-professional football players to ask for their help in raising money. There was the attorney who agreed to handle all the legal documents; the chief financial officer and international consultant who opened the door to Rotarian members made up of numerous business leadership; the priest who was the city's Catholic diocesan administrator; and the devoted wife and partner Cindy Shinsky, without whose support John's dream would have been all but impossible. To this day, John's list of "converts" continues to grow on almost a weekly basis.

When I learned of John's project, I had to ask why he believed such a city could be built. "David," he replied, "who would have thought that an orphan would have been in a position to one day build an orphanage? And could anyone have predicted that this academic all-American football player would give up a chance to play in the NFL for an opportunity to help children with disabilities?" John continued. "And could I have imagined that this 'teacher' would be taught by two elderly sisters on what's important in life? Or that I would attempt to build a 'city of children' in a place where I can't even speak the language?" John's last comment crystallized his vision. "Besides, David, God has been behind me from the beginning. He has come too far to back out now!"

Fortunately for the orphans of Matamoros, Mexico, there is a lovely couple in Dewitt, Michigan, whose friends also say, "We have come too far to back out now."

Something to Ponder

Conviction or Complacency...taking a stand or walking away...having the courage to do what's right or wishing it were so...are the alternatives we are often faced with. Clearly, one cannot be happy playing both sides of the fence. Sooner or later a choice must be made. To help clarify your position, you may want to consider the following questions:

When was the last time someone's complacency made you happy? Are you happy with people who insist they are "entitled" to one thing or another without having to earn that which they cherish? Does a person who won't take a position on right or wrong, good or evil, instill a sense of confidence or trust? Do you know any "happy" cowards? What price would you be willing to pay to obtain happiness in this world if it came at the expense of others? And how many people do you know who are pleased with today's political system, business community, education system, justice system, media, healthcare, religion, and entertainment industry? Finally, can you say with confidence that today's parents have the answers needed to raise moral children in an immoral world?

While you weigh your answers to the above questions, ask yourself what you think the following passage means: "*I know your works; I know that you are neither cold not hot. I wish you were either cold or hot. So, because you are lukewarm, neither hot nor cold, I will spit you out of my mouth*" (Rev. 3: 15–16). Both conviction and complacency have their place in the next world. Which you choose is up to you.

CHOICE #6
PRIDE or PROPER PRIDE

A New Definition

Some years ago I came across a rather interesting phrase that captured a Fortune 500 company's philosophy. ServiceMaster is an international industrial and consumer cleaning product and service organization with headquarters based in Downers Grove, Illinois. Their long-standing reputation for quality, service, profitability, and growth is impressive. One of the reasons for their success is their maxim, "proper pride," which means "to multiply in the lives of others those talents one receives from God."

Where misuse of pride becomes a sin, proper pride may well be the antidote. If we recognize that each of us, regardless of our standing in life, is accountable to do the best we can with what we have been given, are we not doing the work of God? And if our "talents" are multiplied through the actions of others because of what we did for them, have we not made this world a better place? Is not the reverse also true? If we choose not to share our money, talent, and time, what good have we done? The choice is ours: we can die rich or we can die rich in good works.

One of the parables Jesus used to teach the people about the evil of pride described a situation where a religious leader and a tax collector were praying in the temple. The Pharisee was thanking God for not behaving as the rest of men: evildoers, adulterers and sinners. The publican could only beat his breast asking God to have mercy on his soul. Jesus ended His parable with the words, *"I say to you, this man went down into his house justified, rather than the other: because every one that exalteth himself, shall be humbled: and he that humbleth himself, shall be exalted"* (Lk: 28: 9–14).

But sometimes it's not easy to avoid pride. Family talents, success at work, and personal accomplishments (not to mention being in the right place at the right time) have the potential to prompt us to trade humility for arrogance. This behavior can eventually lead to a false realization that the individual is totally responsible for his or her good fortune. In their mind, they are "gifted," not because of what God has blessed them with, but because what they themselves have accomplished. They believe that their success has nothing to do with their Creator, rather, everything to do with what they themselves created. This self-proclaimed self-righteousness will eventually set the stage for failure in their marriage, profession, or life. Narcissism has a way of blinding the fact that what has been given can just as easily be stripped away.

Infamous figures have fallen from power because of their misguided pride. Satan fell like lightning from the heavens because of disobedience and his desire "to be as God." The biblical character King Herod, like the sixteenth-century Ivan the Terrible, both murdered members of their family because of pride and fear that others were plotting against them. And the King of France, Louis XIV (1643–1715), had the gall to ask, "*Has God forgotten all I have done for Him?*"

But the sin of pride is not just reserved for evil men. Saint Peter the Apostle claimed he would never abandon Christ. Three denials later he fled in shame. General George Patton, a World War II military hero, was publicly humiliated at the pinnacle of his career. His flamboyant, arrogant personality eventually fell out of favor with the military brass. A short time later, the general was quoted as saying, "*Success is how high you bounce when you hit bottom.*"

Fortunately there are occasional world leaders who come along in history that magnify the meaning of "proper pride." Such was the case of the late Pope John Paul II. Here was a man whose death stopped the world. According to the Zenit News Agency, 12 million Internet citations and 100,000 media stories flooded communication networks. Not bad for a simple man who was buried in a "pine box."

This man's life story is worth studying. His personal example taught the world about leadership, character, ethics, morals, values, and virtues. But of course there are other choices. If you want to read a book about leadership, you can choose from more than 21,000 titles. Books on character, ethics, morals, values, and virtues are plentiful, with more than 50,000 choices available. And should you want deeper "self help" discussions, there are another 37,600 options to choose from. This "moral math" parallels the more than 32 million laws listed in city, state, and federal directories. Perhaps the nine *Beatitudes* or *Ten Commandments* could provide the answers our society is seeking. Our dependence on worldly wisdom may be the reason why General Omar Bradley once said, "*We have grasped the mystery of the atom and rejected the Sermon on the Mount.*"

I Have The Right...

We all have rights. Take parenting for example. We can sit back and blame teachers for increasing dropouts, poor test scores, or school violence; or get actively involved with our children's education. We have the right to demand that business invest in youth to ensure that it will be easier for our sons and daughters to do better in school; or we can take the responsibility of teaching our children what it means to have a strong work ethic. We can elect politicians who promise to give us better schools; or we can get involved and not wait for bureaucracy to solve our nation's education dilemma. Parents can expect psychologists, authors, and talk show hosts to help raise their children; or they can do their job providing both love and limits. Moms and dads have the right to avoid sex education controversies; but will they have the courage to support abstinence? They can blame other parents for not raising *their* children properly; or focus on their own parental responsibility. We can defend our children from teachers or coaches who demand good performance and behavior; or realize that "victimology" blurs truth.

As parents we have the right to protect our children from church and state violations; or we can demonstrate integrity by supporting the *Ten Commandments*. A father can scream "censorship," protecting freedom of speech and expression; or battle against immoral entertainment. A mother can object to anyone teaching her children the difference between right and wrong; or support authorities who reinforce honesty, compassion, self-discipline and good citizenship. Both parents can teach their children about freedom of choice; but will they support the sanctity of life? Mothers and fathers have the right to decide whether or not to expose their children to religion; but will they accept the responsibility to give their sons and daughters a spiritual foundation?

A few months ago I received an email regarding a California school answering machine message that clearly represents what can happen when parenting pride goes awry. Imagine if your child's school offered the following choices:

"Hello, you have reached the automated answering service of your school. In order to assist you in connecting the right staff member, please listen to all your options before making a selection:

- To lie about why your child is absent—press 1
- To make excuses for why your child did not do their work—press 2
- To complain about what we do—press 3

- To swear at staff members—press 4
- To ask why you didn't get the information listed in your parents newsletter—press 5
- If you want us to raise your child—press 6
- If you want to reach out and touch, slap, or hit someone—press 7
- To request another teacher for the third time this year—press 8
- To complain about bus transportation—press 9
- To complain about school lunches—press 0

If you realize that this is the real world and your child must be accountable for his or her behavior, class work, homework, and that it's not the teachers' fault for your child's lack of effort, hang up and have a nice day!"

This satire was obviously intended to expose parents who blame educators for their own failures. One of the best examples of misguided finger pointing I had ever heard was brought to my attention by my daughter-in-law, Kate. In her city there is a private high school that caters to the children of well-heeled professionals. Tuition rates far exceed those of other private schools. One day school authorities ticketed a number of students for parking their BMW's in a handicapped parking zone. As a result, a number of parents called the principal's office to complain, arguing that they should not have to pay the fines because of the high tuition they pay for their children's education. Unfortunately, news of this episode hit the papers bringing embarrassment to the offenders' parents. Someone once wrote, "*Swallowing your pride seldom leads to indigestion.*" Hopefully these parents and their teenagers have learned the consequences of their behavior.

Remember Me

I have had my fair share of "pride swallowing." After experiencing Mel Gibson's film, *The Passion of the Christ*, I was haunted by the way this award winning director drew our attention to the temple guard who lost his ear in an altercation with the apostle Peter; or Pilate's wife whose kindness was extended to the victim's mother; and Simon of Cyrene, the reluctant volunteer, who ended up defending the Savior. I will forever remember the Roman soldier whose expression confirmed that he had just executed the Son of God. And who will forget the condemned thief who pleaded, "*Jesus, remember me when you come into your kingdom*" (Lk 24: 42).

After seeing the film I couldn't help but wonder how many lost souls would be affected by the experience. Like the Pharisee in the temple who was proud that he wasn't like other men, I began to mock other sinners that likely saw the movie. I just knew there were so-called Catholic politicians whose pro-abortion position fell apart when Mary stared into the camera holding her crucified Son. And of course there must have been parents present who suddenly realized that the children they were blessed with were gifts from God. My private ranting continued as I knew judges guilty of anti-Christian decisions must have seen the film. I also imagined that Hollywood producers avoided the screening because they were too busy filming their next pornographic movie. My "soul targeting" went on with the belief that more than one Chief Executive Officer was uncomfortable with the corruption between Jerusalem's elite. Perhaps, I pondered, a newspaper movie critic assigned to cover the film struggled with the words, "*What is Truth?*" Surely he wasn't alone as more than one lawyer must have squirmed at the same scene.

I had more questions. Did anyone notice a member of the clergy whose discomfort with the film's message had everything to do with what he failed to do? Could one draw a parallel with sports celebrities and their agents to the thirty pieces of silver? And did intellectuals and scholars see themselves in the role of the Pharisees? Were prostitutes, drug addicts, alcoholics, and abortion mill nurses present? And did the movie "prick" at their conscience? My sarcasm culminated with a self-righteous prediction that the churches would be filled to capacity in the coming months.

After blaming other sinners for crucifying Jesus, it dawned on me: Like them, I was equally or even more responsible for the passion of Christ; I who complain when asked to carry a cross the weight of a "toothpick;" or fail to recognize the cross that others carry; or worse yet, refuse to help those who struggle with their cross. It was easy to condemn my fellow movie patrons while forgetting what I had failed to do. Suddenly, the phrase "remember me," pierced my soul. It was then I began to realize that these two simple words represented not only what I ask of Jesus: but what the Son of God asks of me. At that hour, "proper pride" had saved the day.

British writer and Christian apologist C.S. Lewis (1898–1963) said it best: "*A proud man is always looking down on things and people; and of course, as long as you're looking down, you can't see something that's above you.*"

The "7" Gifts

In Catholic teaching there are seven supernatural gifts of the Holy Spirit that are strengthened in candidates at the administration of the Sacrament of Confirmation. These gifts are *fear of the Lord, piety, knowledge, fortitude, counsel, understanding*, and *wisdom*. Each gift is recognized as a special grace to receive divine inspirations. Like "proper pride," they offer the opportunity to multiply in the lives of others those talents (gifts) one receives from God. The following stories reveal the power of each:

The Diary—During the Revolutionary War a British officer got separated from his unit. Realizing that the Continental Army was nearby, he carefully moved through the forest hoping to remain undetected. The officer came to a small clearing where he saw another military leader on his knees with head bowed. Moving closer he realized that the man praying was wearing a Continental Army uniform. He silently listened to his prayers. Sometime later, the British officer found his way back to his unit and headed straight for his tent. He pulled out his diary and made the following notation. *"When I saw the sight, I knew we were defeated. For any army whose commander was so humble before almighty God could never lose the war."* The commander the officer was referring to was General George Washington! This future American President understood what it meant to have "fear of the Lord" as he trusted in the will of God by demonstrating a special reverence for his Creator.

Got a Minute?—When I was in Catholic elementary school, all students had to attend daily Mass at the noon hour. Every day at precisely 12:05 p.m., a young man would come into the back of the church, kneel down, beat his breast, and whisper, *"Lord, I've only got a minute. I love you."* He would then jump up, run out the back door, and head down the street. This ritual would happen day after day, week after week. No one seemed to know who he was. One day, Fr. Barry got an emergency call from a local plant manager who explained that there had been a horrible accident. The man involved was asking for a priest. Fr. Barry raced to the plant and discovered that the mortally injured worker was the same stranger who visited the church every day at noon. At the moment last rites were administered, the young man looked straight ahead, smiled, and said, *"Lord, I'll see you in a minute."* With that, he closed his eyes and died. His love for God was manifested in the gift of piety.

The Humble Intellectual—She was an orthodox Jew. She was highly intelligent. And she was an avowed atheist. Born Edith Stein, she died Sister Theresa Benedicta of the Cross at the hands of the Nazis in the Auschwitz concentration camp. Her journey to martyrdom came with the gift of "knowledge" as her faith revealed the truth she was so desperately seeking. Her awakening began the day after she visited Anna Reinach, the widow of a favorite professor who had been killed in battle. Edith believed she was to play a role as consoler, but was shocked to discover that Anna's Christian faith was the only comfort she needed. Edith's life began to change. She studied the lives of the saints, was baptized, and later became a Carmelite nun. Four years later she was arrested by the Gestapo and eventually died in a gas chamber. Edith once wrote, "'Thy will be done,' must be the rule of Christian life." For Sister Theresa Benedicta of the Cross, the knowledge of God's will for her life, and death, was all she needed.

No Greater Love—Maximilian Kolbe was also highly intelligent. His penchant for math, physics, and space flight was second only to his love for God. Founder of the Knights of Immaculata, a ministry dedicated to the salvation of souls, he would be especially remembered for his personal sacrifice on behalf of others. When Fr. Kolbe was beaten repeatedly by an S.S. Officer, his adversary had a difficult time understanding where his victim got such perseverance. When this humble priest asked the German Commandant to allow him to take the place of a condemned man, fellow prisoners were shocked. When Fr. Kolbe was thrown in the starvation bunker with nine others, the guards were stunned to hearing singing and praying instead of crying and moaning. What the Nazis failed to realize was that Fr. Kolbe had the gift of "fortitude" which gave him the grace to overcome fear, pain, and suffering. In the Gospel of John, chapter 15, verse 13, Jesus said, "*No one has greater love than this, to lay down one's life for one's friends.*" Fr. Kolbe understood this passage. He also understood the gift of "fortitude."

Man's Search for Meaning—Another story from Auschwitz came years after the war was over. Victor Frankl was a Jewish psychiatrist who lost his mother, father, wife, and children in the dreaded concentration camp. Fourteen years after the end of World War II, Frankl wrote a book entitled, *Man's Search For Meaning*. His runaway bestseller captured the unbelievable acts of horror perpetrated on the residents of that infamous prison. Story after story demonstrated the power of the human spirit during the worst conditions imaginable. One character Frankl introduced to his readership was a man who was freezing to death. Lying on a cement slab in the middle of winter, the dying man tells Frankl that though the

Nazis had killed his family, stolen his dignity, and ruined his health, he would never surrender his attitude. As Frankl wrote, "*The way in which a man accepts his fate and all the suffering it entails, the way in which he takes up his cross, gives him ample opportunity—even under the most difficult circumstances—to add a deeper meaning to his life.*" God gave Victor Frankl the gift of "counsel" allowing him to communicate the differences between good and evil, despair and hope, sorrow and joy.

The Sign—A number of years ago I had the honor of hearing the story of a very successful executive who experienced the gift of "understanding." As the top salesman for his company, John was offered the opportunity to start a new division in the educational field. After accepting the assignment he immediately began marketing the program to school superintendents. He made sales calls. He attended trade shows. He advertised in trade journals. For months he tried every technique possible but failed to land a single client. Depression was beginning to cloud his optimism. He called his secretary to make an appointment with the CEO. He intended to resign his position. The meeting was set for Thursday. Three days before that, a friend called and invited John to a superintendent meeting. "Who knows," his friend opined, "you may meet someone who will help you break into the educational business." Reluctantly, John agreed to attend the statewide educational meeting. The weather was terrible that evening and getting worse. After parking the car he crossed the street heading toward the convention hall when all of a sudden a stranger was standing in the middle of the road. As John stated, "I don't understand how I never noticed him from the other side of the street. It was almost as if he suddenly appeared." The man standing before John said nothing, only offering his hand. John told me he rarely gave money to "street" people. But for some reason he stopped, took out his wallet, and handed the stranger five dollars. The intruder nodded his approval and without saying anything he handed what John thought was a business card. John looked at the card and discovered that it only listed sign language symbols used by people who were deaf and couldn't speak.

He stuck the card in his shirt pocket and walked into the convention hall. For the umpteenth time the experience was the same. Not a single superintendent was interested in either John's services or John himself. He left the meeting a beaten man. Later that evening in the privacy of his apartment, he broke down and cried out to God. "Lord, I've failed. And come tomorrow I'm going to admit my failure. But if this is a business I can serve you in, I need a sign."

The following morning, John was heading to the CEO's office when his secretary stopped him in the hallway to show her boss a Sunday newspaper from a large East Coast city. Simultaneously another manager, who had just returned from the West Coast, came up to John and handed him a newspaper from a major city in California. The manager, like John's secretary, had circled an advertisement. John looked at both papers, smiled, turned to his secretary and said, "Martha, cancel my appointment with the CEO. There is business waiting for us." I asked John how he knew. "David," he said, "both advertisements were asking for suppliers to submit a 'request for proposal' in the very service line I was desperately trying to sell." "But John," I interrupted, "how did you know that this was the sign you asked for?" John smiled. "David, both advertisements were sponsored by schools for the deaf!"

The gift of understanding provides a deep insight into the will of God. As Fr. William Saunders in his article, "Gifts of the Holy Spirit" commented, "*This gift brings the virtue of faith to perfection.*" And because of his faith, John is now multiplying in the lives of others those talents he has received from God.

The Little Way—St. Therese of Lisieux died in a convent at age twenty-four. Shortly after her death, her sister Pauline sent copies of the young saint's writings to other convents throughout France. In a very short time, hundreds of thousands of copies were ordered by people around the world who wanted to achieve holiness. In 1925, just twenty-eight years after her death, Therese was canonized a saint. And in 1997, Pope John Paul the II made Saint Therese of Lisieux a *Doctor of the Church*, an honor bestowed on special saints who are recognized as outstanding teachers of the Catholic faith. Today, over 1 million visitors come annually to her shrine in France; her only book, *Story of a Soul* (published after her death), is still in demand; and a new movie on her life has been released.

How is it that a person, with no degree in theology, who lived the last eight years of her life in a convent, and died before her twenty-fifth birthday, could achieve such honors? St. Therese was given the gift of wisdom allowing her to communicate, in a very simple way, what's important to God. In life she prayed that God would grant her the privilege to work on behalf of earthly souls long after she entered the gates of Heaven. Clearly, He heard her prayers as she continues to multiply in the lives of others those gifts she received from God.

The Highest Honor

When I was preparing to write this chapter, I asked myself what vocation best exemplifies the spirit of "proper pride?" Easy choices might include missionaries, Red Cross volunteers, hospice workers, or members of the Peace Corps. Then I came across an interesting commentary on the history and protocols of the guards that watch over the *"Tomb of the Unknown Soldier."* These gentlemen must fall within certain height and weight limits, live two years in special accommodations located beneath the tomb, avoid alcohol or swearing, and study the lives of those laid to rest in Arlington National Cemetery.

What I found most interesting was their commitment to duty. When Hurricane Isabelle approached the shores of Washington, D. C. in 2003, the city's politicians and government workers took two days off. But when the tomb's guards were given permission to suspend their assignment, every man in the unit refused to abandon his post. Because of their fidelity to duty, the *Tomb of the Unknown Soldier* has been guarded around the clock for over seventy-five years.

We don't have to join a unique military unit to demonstrate "proper pride." All that's necessary is to do our best with the talents we have; not for personal gain, but for the glory of God. So whether you work at Arlington National Cemetery, 1600 Pennsylvania Avenue, or 123 Main Street, your duty is the same: To multiply in the lives of others those talents you have received from God.

Something to Ponder

Do you believe in coincidence, serendipity, or just plain luck? There are some individuals in this world that seem to have everything fall in place. I know one such young man who is continually blessed with good fortune. As a sophomore in college, my son Andrew was invited to a special meeting with the deans of the economic school for a private discussion regarding the last wishes of a major donor. This meeting eventually led to an educational grant, a high-paying internship, his first job in the most exciting city in the world, and marriage to a lovely lady named Julie. Two years after fulfilling his CPA requirements with the international accounting firm, KPMG, Andrew was recruited to join a young company that offered unlimited potential. Three weeks into the new job he happened to be on the same elevator with the president of the firm. This gentleman turned to Andrew and said, "I understand you went to high school in Ohio." "Yessir, I graduated from Walsh Jesuit in Stow, Ohio." my son responded. "Your kidding."

came the reply. "I am the current Chairman of the Board for Walsh Jesuit High School!" And so it goes for this twenty-six-year-old young man.

Those who know Andrew will often mention his talent, intellect, and charisma. Yes, he has all of these. But he has something else yet to be discovered. Andrew has the responsibility to multiply in the lives of others those gifts he has received from God.

And that's the way it is for many of us. We are so caught up in accomplishments and goals that we forget we have a greater calling. Further, we too often take for granted our state in life. As an exercise, list on the left side of a piece of paper all that you have been blessed with. On the right side of the same piece of paper, make a list of all the things that could have happened to you (from the hour you were born to the present day) that would have made your life more challenging. Hopefully, your latter documentation is at least twice as long as your former list. If not, then I wonder if you took into account the following realities: unemployment, poverty, war, crime, sickness, loneliness, despair, broken vows, broken homes, broken hearts, children or siblings who are ill, handicapped, or in trouble, parents or grandparents with debilitating disease or dementia, and finally, a lack of a spiritual foundation to help cope with life's uncertainties.

"But for the grace of God go I," is a prayer I say daily to remind my pride that were it not for God's mercy, there's no telling how unhappy my life would be. And to ensure that I have every opportunity to experience eternal happiness, it is imperative that all I have, all I do, all I say, and all I am, is devoted to the greater glory of God.

That said, I invite you to return to your piece of paper and create a third column. This time jot down all you intend to do each day to demonstrate the gift of "proper pride." Follow your plan, and you are well on your way to finding the eternal happiness you seek. Or as Victor Frankl put it, *"Everything can be taken from man but one thing: the last of human freedoms—to choose one's own attitude in any set of circumstances, to choose one's own way."*

CHOICE #7
FORGIVENESS or
CONDEMNATION

HUMAN OR DIVINE?

Author Alexander Pope penned the famous phrase, *"To err is human, to forgive divine."* Unfortunately when it comes to forgiveness, human weakness often rules the day. When someone hurts us, we find it very easy to condemn that individual for what he or she has done. Even when they say they are sorry, our ability to forget their transgressions is often a monumental task. When a person is inconsiderate, we find it very difficult to tolerate their presence. Should they slander our name, the desire for revenge comes too easily. Lying, cheating, and stealing are particularly difficult to forgive, much less forget. After all, how can you trust someone you can't turn your back on? It's so easy to write off a selfish, insensitive, belligerent, disrespectful, vindictive, or abrasive individual. If you are embarrassed by a friend, family member, or fellow worker, it may take a long time before you can bring yourself to forget what they did. And should you be betrayed by those closest to you, forgiveness may seem all but impossible.

Though Kin Hubbard's humorous comment that, *"Nobody forgets where they buried the hatchet,"* may have some merit, the real question is: Can a person be unforgiving and truly be happy at the same time?

Was it Jesus' human or divine nature that drove Him to cry out from the cross, *"Father, forgive them, they know not what they do"* (Lk 23: 33–34). Look at how He suffered at the hands of His executioners. How could any innocent human being possibly forgive those who took such delight in torturing their victim? And yet, there have been many martyrs who prayed for their enemies and tormentors.

One of the best examples is Saint Maria Goretti. A few days before her twelfth birthday, she was viciously attacked by a nineteen-year-old man whose fury was driven by Maria's refusal to have sexual relations with him. Stabbed fourteen times, Maria died after suffering excruciating pain for over twenty hours. Moments before her death, the priest who was administering last rites asked Maria if she could forgive her assassin. The young girl replied, "*Yes, for the love of Jesus I forgive him...and I want him to be with me in paradise. May God forgive him because I have already forgiven him.*" With those final words she died on July 6, 1902.

Other saints have suffered at the hands of fellow Christians. Their particular plight called for a special grace needed to forgive their perpetrators. Saint John of the Cross, author of *Dark Night of the Soul*, was imprisoned in a six-foot by ten-foot cell by Carmelite priests because they were uncomfortable with the reforms he suggested for their order. For nine months he was beaten and forced to live in silence. He was later vindicated by church authorities.

Saint John Vianney was ridiculed by other seminarians because of his struggles to master his studies. After his ordination, the bishop told him that he would not be allowed to hear confessions at his parish until his understanding of moral theology improved. This decision was a humiliating blow for the new priest. Still, he remained obedient to his superiors and held no ill will against them. Eventually he received permission to administer the Sacrament of Reconciliation. Shortly thereafter, his reputation for holiness and ability to read souls spread all over France. Today, Saint John Vianney is the patron saint of Catholic priests worldwide.

Saint Padre Pio's mystical gifts got him in trouble with the local archbishop and other jealous priests who accused this humble man of cavorting with Satan. After all, his adversaries argued, how could a simple priest read souls, heal the infirmed, be seen in two places at the same time, or experience the stigmata (the wounds of Christ)? Because of these accusations he was forbidden to say Mass publicly or hear confessions for six years. Eventually all charges were dropped, and the Archbishop who accused Padre Pio was removed from office.

In the prologue of this book I mentioned the film *Song of Bernadette*. There is a scene in the movie where Bernadette, now a religious sister, is tormented by one of the other nuns in the convent who is extremely jealous of the visionary from Lourdes. Bernadette's response to this troubled nun is a wonderful example of compassion. In one particular exchange, the doubting sister asks Bernadette to prove that her continued limping is not an excuse to gain attention. Bernadette lovingly shows the sister the bone cancer that has been slowly killing her. Horrified, the startled nun rushes out of Bernadette's room to the chapel where she falls on the floor in tears begging Christ to forgive her for mistreating the future saint. As Bernadette's cancer progresses, she eventually needs assistance to help her get around the convent. In a later scene, the same nun who caused so much mental suffering for Bernadette is now at her side twenty-four hours a day caring for the needs of the dying sister.

Bernadette's kindness, compassion, and forgiveness are examples all of us can use when tempted to judge others. Bernadette was not divine, but the gifts she gave were divinely inspired.

Back to Dante

Let's return one last time to Dante's *Divine Comedy*. In the *Inferno*, the poet and his guide Virgil travel to Hell by descending down nine circles of torment where one lost soul after another suffers. With each new encounter, Dante and Virgil witness greater and greater evil and their corresponding punishments.

Imagine a modern day scenario where you're asked to visit nine unhappy people who have offended you at one time or another. Imagine further that their eternal salvation depends on your willingness to forgive them. Could you:

1. Forgive the colleague from work whose complacency on a sensitive issue left you holding the bag, as you tried to defend your position before management?

2. Forgive the person whose inappropriate sexual behavior made you, or someone you respected, very uncomfortable?

3. Forgive the brother whose uncontrollable desire for food and alcohol is an embarrassment to you and your family?

4. Forgive the family miser who hoards everything within grasp, refusing to share anything with you or those you love?

5. Forgive the out-of-control individual whose anger and threats leave you with worry and fear?

6. Forgive the "heretic" who talks out of two sides of her mouth resulting in unnecessary dissent?

7. Forgive the violent individual who personally harms you or a member of your family?

8. Forgive the person who steals from you, lies about you, or whose fraudulent behavior results in their personal gain at your personal loss?

9. Forgive the traitor whose treachery leads to disloyalty and hatred between husbands and wives, brothers and sisters, friends and neighbors, or coworkers and colleagues?

If you had trouble forgiving one or more of these fictitious souls, then change the scene and put yourself on one of the crosses to either the right or left of the dying Christ. Would you have hesitated to ask for His mercy? If the answer to the question is too obvious, then ask yourself how many times your spouse, parent, child, best friend, long-time neighbor, teacher, coach, or coworker, has asked you for forgiveness?

If the shoe were on the other foot, would you expect them to forgive you? If your salvation depended upon their forgiveness, would you not beg for mercy? And what would you do if you discovered that your choice to condemn others resulted in God's choice to condemn you? Said another way, if you believe that eternal happiness is predicated on God's mercy, then why would you not be merciful to others?

In the parable of the unforgiving servant, Jesus relates a story to the Apostle Peter about a king who forgave the debt of one of his workers. That same man refused to forgive a much smaller debt owed him by one of his servants. When the king learned about this lack of compassion, he summoned the evil servant and demanded to know why, after receiving mercy from the king, he did not show mercy to others? In the end the unforgiving servant was punished. Jesus' warning was clear: *"So will my heavenly Father do to you, unless each of you forgives his brother from his heart"* (Mt 18:35).

The Father I Never Knew

At the beginning of this book I made a casual reference to my father. I have reserved the story of our relationship, or lack thereof, until now. As I mentioned earlier, my mother divorced my father when I was six months old. From the time we left Wisconsin until my teenage years, I never heard his voice, received a letter from him, or even saw a picture of my dad. At age sixteen I talked to my father for the first time.

It was a typical Saturday morning and I was getting ready to go out and play ball with my friends. Just before I walked out the door, the telephone rang. Pausing for a moment, I waited to see if the call was for me. After speaking briefly with the caller my mother handed me the phone and said matter-of-factly, "Your father is on the line." Stunned, I hesitated for a few seconds and then took the phone. "Hello." "This is your father," was the reply. His words nearly knocked the wind out of me. "Hi D—." My poor attempt to get the "D" word out must have been evident to the man on the other end of the line. "Son," he continued, "I wanted to get in touch with you to let you know that I think of you quite often." I remained silent. "Perhaps you could drop me a line or give me a call sometime," he pleaded. By this time my mother had walked into the other room leaving a father and his son to their privacy. "I guess I could do that," I stammered. After a few more minutes of one-way conversation we hung up. My mother never did ask what he said. It didn't matter much anyways, as I wouldn't speak to my dad for another seven years.

I never had a natural curiosity about my father. My mother never talked about him and I never bothered to ask what he was like, how he looked, what he did for a living, or the more difficult question, what happened? I just accepted the fact that I was destined to grow up without a dad. On occasion some friends or their parents would inquire if I missed not having a father-figure in my life. I could only respond, "It's like ice cream. If you never taste it, you don't miss it."

On May 26, 1970, four days after my marriage to Cindy, we received a wedding gift from my father. After the initial shock, it dawned on me that my mom had called my dad's mother to inform her that her grandson had just got married. And because of her action, I had no choice. I had to call him. From that moment on we exchanged phone "pleasantries" on Father's Day and Christmas.

Four years later, a week before Thanksgiving, I received another stranger's call. Her name was Mary and she was my half sister. I knew that my father had remarried and had three other children, two boys and a girl. "David," she began, "The family would like to invite you and Cindy to come up to Wisconsin, to celebrate the Thanksgiving holiday." Though I was unprepared for this second invitation, I was more mature and immediately accepted.

The day before Cindy and I left to travel to the dairy state, I received a second call from Mary. She informed me that there had been a change of plans. My dad didn't want to meet his son. Taken back, I immediately demanded to know why. Mary said, "David, please understand. Your dad wants to see you but he can't get over the fact that each of his children has had trouble in their lives, whereas, the son he never raised has a master's degree, is married, and has a good job." "But Mary," I countered, "who I am should have nothing to do with the fact that it's time for a father and son to meet." "Nevertheless," she responded, "the time is not right."

CHOICE #7 FORGIVENESS or CONDEMNATION

That time would come nine years later when Mary called a third time. "David, remember me?" she asked. Somewhat reserved I responded, "Oh hello, Mary, what's up?" "Well, the time is right for you to visit your dad." "Mary," I retorted, "we've been down this road before." "Yes, I know," she said meekly. "But this time things are different. Dad lives alone and his health is not good. He keeps hoping that the day will come when he will have a chance to meet his first-born son before he dies." Somewhat angry I asked, "And just how should we arrange this meeting?" "David," Mary said, "you just have to take the initiative and come up to Wisconsin." She went on. "But it's important that you don't tell him you're coming because he won't be able to handle the stress." Oh sure, I thought, I'll just walk up to his door, ring the bell, and when he answers, I'll say, "Hi, Dad, how have you been these past thirty-six years?" I finished my conversation with Mary promising to give her invitation some thought.

A month later I was in Chicago on a business trip and decided to give my father a call. "Dad, how are you doing?" I asked. "Fine, son," was his reply. I immediately proceeded to inform him that I would be flying into LaCrosse, Wisconsin, arriving about 4:00 p.m., and that I hoped he would be there to meet me at the airport. With obvious shock he said, "I'll be there." I wasn't convinced that he would be at the gate when I arrived.

When I got off the plane, I waited till all the passengers had either met their loved ones or scurried off to their next destination. For a moment I thought I was the only person in the waiting lounge. Suddenly my eye caught the image of a stocky gentleman dressed in overalls and wearing a big farmer's hat. NO, I thought, surely he wasn't my father. Slowly the stranger came up to the unclaimed visitor. "You must be my father," I stated. "And you must be my son," he responded; thus began a twenty-four-hour visit to catch up on thirty-six years.

I immediately got a taste of the world I never knew when we got in his pick-up truck. The gun rack did nothing to settle my stomach. As we pulled into his driveway, the rising garage door unveiled a history I never understood. My dad had every tool Sears and Roebuck ever sold. I didn't have the heart to tell him that his son was a mechanical idiot. As we got out of the truck, he led me around to the back of his house. "Wait till you see my garden," he said. Behind his two-bedroom bungalow I discovered row after row of vegetable plots. I silently prayed that corn, or pork and beans, would be on the evening's menu. He would never learn that his son used to wait until his mother turned her back before picking anything "green" off his plate, which he would later deposit in the weeds.

Over the next day we got to know each other. I discovered that, like his son, he spent a number of years in the Air Force. I also learned that he too was left-handed just like his grandson, Andrew. Both pitched for their baseball teams. More important, we both learned that there was no animosity on my part for the father I never knew. I saw my dad two more times before he died. At the funeral home I finally met Mary and my two half brothers. All of them welcomed me to the family.

It would have been very easy for me to condemn my dad for waiting so long before he reached out to his son. But who was I to question what he did or failed to do? Would I have been happier growing up with a father? Who is to say? For whatever reason, I grew up in a single-parent home. I never wanted for anything. I never got into trouble. And somehow, someway, I managed to turn out ok. For these reasons, it was not my place to expect my father to ask for forgiveness. On the contrary, it was my responsibility to share a memory of my father with his grandchildren. In an odd way, I may have my dad to thank for helping me realize how important a father is in the lives of children. And though I never experienced happy times that many sons and daughters have with their dad, nor did I experience the sad times that often go with the relationship.

For whatever reason, God decided that I would grow up in a single-parent home. I could have complained. I could have used the lack of a father's love as a "crutch" in life. I could have used my personal situation as a poor excuse for being a poor father. I could have chosen to be unhappy, blaming everything and everyone for what I did not have. I did none of these. Instead, I accepted who I was and the blessings I did have. For at the end of my life, the only thing that will be important is what I did with the gifts I was given. Furthermore, how could I condemn a man I never knew?

The Man Who Condemned God

Larry Vuillemin had it all: Loving parents, athletic ability, good looks, and a keen intellect. As an all-state high school football player, there was no doubt he would follow in his brother's footsteps, attending Notre Dame on a full scholarship. Life was good. Then one day Larry's perfect world was shattered. His dad, at age forty-eight, dropped dead of a heart attack. During those early days of mourning, Larry questioned God as to how He could take a church-going man, loving husband, and father from his family.

Shortly after graduating as valedictorian from Notre Dame, Larry learned that another hero was taken from him. His older brother, who had just signed a contract to play professional football, had been diagnosed with schizophrenia. This second tragedy would soon be followed by Larry's broken marriage. In his eyes, God was to blame for all the adversities in his life.

At age thirty-six and already a successful prosecuting attorney, Larry didn't need anyone, especially God. Then one day, while arguing a case in court, he suffered a stroke and collapsed. After crying out from his hospital bed, "God, help me," Larry soon was visited by a Catholic priest who gave Larry the best advice he ever received. "Larry," Fr. Norm Douglas said, "the time has come for you to realize that the God whom you blame for all your misfortunes is the same God who sent His only Son to be crucified so that sinners like you receive the mercy of Christ." Larry became a changed man.

Less than two years after his illness, Larry and Fr. Norm started an organization called *Heart to Heart Communications* whose purpose is to encourage spiritual development in the workplace. For over twenty years, these two gentlemen have touched the souls of thousands of business men and women. And Larry will tell you that many of these professionals share personal crucifixion and resurrection stories that mirror his own. When that happens, Larry Vuillemin can only smile knowing that the God he once condemned is the same God who has forgiven him.

The story of Larry Vuillemin and *Heart to Heart Communications* is a perfect example of what Helen Keller believed when she said, "*When one door of happiness closes, another opens; but often we look so long at the closed door that we do not see the one which has opened for us.*" Helen and Larry have much in common. Both individuals experienced blindness, hers physical, his spiritual. Both had a teacher who believed in them. And both are shining examples of the mercy of God.

Anyway

A number of years ago I came across a simple poem that was attributed to Mother Teresa entitled, *Anyway*. The following words represent a tapestry of her life:

-Anyway-

People are unreasonable, illogical, and self-centered...
Love Them Anyway
If you do good, people will accuse you of selfish, ulterior motives...
Do Good Anyway
If you are successful, you win false friends and enemies...

Succeed Anyway
The good you do will be forgotten tomorrow...
Do Good Anyway
Honesty and frankness make you vulnerable...
Be Honest and Frank Anyway
What you spend years building may be destroyed overnight...
Build Anyway
People really need help but may attack if you help them...
Help People Anyway
Give the world the best you have and you'll get kicked in the teeth...
Give The World The Best You've Got Anyway

Mother Teresa's message could have easily been scripted to communicate the grace of forgiveness. People have their own motives which may or may not recognize the good you try to do. They can accuse you falsely or falsely claim that they are your friends. There will be individuals who never give you credit for what you have accomplished, or worse yet take the credit themselves. And when you tell the truth you may be criticized for your honesty. Be prepared to see others destroy your dream even if it was intended to help them. For at the end of the day only you will know if you have done your best. Even so, be prepared to experience the sins of envy, avarice, pride, sloth, and wrath from those you love. And rather than condemn them for their actions, have faith that your gift of "forgiveness" will be rewarded.

In the sixteenth century there was a priest who lived in Venice, Italy, named Fr. Jerome Emiliani, who built six orphanages, a hospital, and a home for former prostitutes. He died attending to victims of a plague that was ravishing Europe. One of his best sayings parallels the spirit of Mother Teresa's message. *"If you remain constant in the face of trial, the Lord will give you peace and rest for a time in this world, and forever in the next."*

Something to Ponder

Earlier in this chapter I asked whether or not you could forgive a number of fictitious souls for their offense against you. Now I'm going to ask a more difficult question. As you reflect over the wrongs of your past life, do you believe that your own sins are worthy of forgiveness? If someone had done to you what you did to others, could you blame them for condemning your behavior? Should they forgive the times when you acted as judge and jury, poisoned them with your words, lost control in your anger, complained about everyone and everything, were hostile and bitter, filled with self-interest, or suspicious of others' good fortune.

As you examine your conscience, can you honestly say these were happy times? Can you recall an incident when someone you loved accepted your apology? Did you not breathe a sigh of relief? Was not a weight lifted off your shoulders? And haven't you experienced the reverse situation when your willingness to forgive was rewarded with gratefulness?

How many times have you whispered the Lord's prayer? What you probably remember is the line, "and forgive us our trespasses as we forgive our trespassers." But do you also remember what Jesus said to His apostles after he taught them how to pray? His warning was clear: *"If you forgive others their transgressions. Your heavenly Father will forgive you. But if you do not forgive others, neither will your Father forgive your transgressions" (Mt 6: 14).*

If happiness is your destination, then forgiveness is your passport. Or as a sixteenth-century English poet said, *"He that cannot forgive others, breaks the bridge over which he himself must pass if he would ever reach Heaven; for every one has need to be forgiven."* Choose wisely. Your eternity depends on it.

THE CALLING

Strangers

If I've heard it once, I've heard it a hundred times. "Why did you never become a priest?" I could respond with a single word—Cindy—or I could honestly say that the thought never entered my mind. In either case, my decision did not preclude a personal search for my calling in life.

Sometimes I wish that I was a professional golfer, but unless I lower my handicap twenty-five strokes this won't happen. Other times I wish I could sing professionally. That vocation goes down the drain the moment I exit the shower. Though it's fun to escape reality, it's not very productive.

Like many folks, I have changed my career path a number of times. My experience in the Air Force led me to explore a job as an air traffic controller. That opportunity crashed the day my wife of eight months handed me an article that identified the high pressure position as leading the nation in heart attack, divorce, and suicide rates. After my military service, I landed a position as a scheduler for a division of General Motors. This purchasing career came to a screeching halt when the director of the department learned that the study I did for my master's thesis was published in a national magazine. His prodding led to a new opportunity in automotive research which eventually led to a marketing position in the health care industry. Even today I occasionally reflect on what might have been had I stayed with General Motors. But I was meant to follow a different path.

Sometimes the journey we choose has nothing to do with our desires and everything to do with the will of God. One minute you're quite content with the world, and the next minute someone comes into your space to remind you what's really important. I learned this difficult lesson one evening just days before Christmas. At that time I was working on my graduate degree at Wayne State University in downtown Detroit. Before heading to class I often took the time to visit a chapel located on the corner of the campus. On this particular evening I decided that a prayer or two was necessary before I took my final exams. Because it was the dinner hour, the church was empty.

After settling down for a private reflection, I sensed someone looking at me. Turning around, I discovered a young man about thirty-years-old standing twenty feet away. Feeling uneasy, I shifted my briefcase to the inside of the pew. "Is there anything I can help you with?" I asked. The stranger responded almost immediately. "Perhaps you can. You see I just drove into town with my wife and newborn son, and we don't have any place to stay." Recognizing a scam in progress, I asked, "And just where is your wife and son?" "They are in a car parked in front of the church," he replied. I didn't believe his story. I didn't trust his intentions. And I wasn't about to turn my back on him. "Listen," I said, "why don't you go next door to the rectory and ring the door bell. I'm sure the parish priest will have the necessary contacts to help you, your wife, and newborn son." I tried to disguise my sarcasm. The stranger smiled and thanked me for the suggestion.

I turned around again to face the altar. But because I was unsettled with the encounter, I immediately looked over my shoulder to ensure that he was heading to the church's parking lot. The only problem was, he was GONE! Jumping up from the pew, I ran to the back of the church to see where he was hiding. He wasn't anywhere to be found. I ran outside. There was no car, no wife, no baby, no stranger. He had vanished.

I hurried back to the pew, grabbed my briefcase and rushed off to class. Though the instructor ensured the students that the exam would be relatively easy for those who studied, I couldn't concentrate. The questions were competing with the encounter I experienced fifteen minutes earlier. Over and over again I replayed what he said, what I said, and how he seemed to literally disappear. Before class ended I said a silent prayer. "Lord, I don't know what I experienced tonight. But I'm troubled. If the stranger was you in any way, please give me a sign." When class ended, six of us left together and proceeded to where we parked our cars. I said nothing about my experience. As we approached the parking deck, we noticed a homeless man sitting on the curb. He was shivering with the cold. Just before I could pass him, he stood up, stepped in front of me, and said, "Could you spare some change for a warm cup of coffee? But you don't have to touch my unclean hands, just throw your coins in the gutter." I was shaking as I reached for my wallet hoping I had enough cash to settle my debt.

A short time later I had a private conversation with a priest to retell the entire story. He paused a few minutes and then asked, "David, did you say that this stranger mentioned that he, his wife, and newborn son, had just arrived in town?" "Yes, Father." I responded timidly. "And did you say that he told you he had no place to go?" I could only nod. "And this experience happened just before Christmas, is that correct?" I knew where he was going. "Son," he said solemnly, "you were the innkeeper that night, and there was no room in your heart." His words stung my soul.

I have shared that story countless times. On more than one occasion it has been suggested by others that my "calling" was meant to happen. Their logic suggests that I was chosen so that others would think twice before they reject those in need. To this day I can't help but think what might have happened had I reached out to the visitor who suddenly came into my life.

Sometimes we think we understand what our calling is, only to learn that God has another agenda. On one particular occasion, I was asked to give a presentation to a chapter of the American Marketing Association in Akron, Ohio. Surprisingly my host suggested that rather than speak about health care marketing, I share with the audience my involvement in the *Back to the Family* project sponsored by Children's Medical Center of Akron. Though flattered, I had to ask, "How does a message on parenting fit with the educational interests of your membership?" "David," the executive director said, "because the meeting falls on Valentine's Day, we have invited everyone to bring their spouse or significant other to hear your humorous and emotional talk.

On the night of the presentation, I was preparing to go on stage when I noticed a college instructor enter the room with about fifteen of his marketing students. As I learned later, this professor required his students to attend the monthly association meeting so they could learn something about their chosen career field. When I saw them take their seats, I couldn't help but think that I was about to disappoint at least ten percent of my audience.

I spoke for about an hour, after which I received a nice round of applause. Gathering my materials I proceeded to exit the banquet room when I noticed a young student heading in my direction. Oh-oh, I thought, here comes a dissatisfied customer. "Mr. Eich, have you got a minute?" the young man inquired. Preparing for an unfavorable critique, I began to explain why my presentation had nothing to do with marketing. "No-no, you don't understand," he interrupted. "I want to thank you for what you did this evening." Puzzled, I let him continue. "You see, Mr. Eich, though I didn't learn anything about my area of study, you taught me something much more important. It has been four weeks since I called my mom and dad and your message reminded me that I have the responsibility to tell my parents how much I love them." He went on. "And tonight, they are going to hear from their son!"

I have had the honor of speaking to a number of groups around the country on a variety of topics. I have been humbled to receive standing ovations, letters of appreciation, and many public and private endorsements. But before that evening I had never been so moved, knowing that God selected me to reach someone who was lost. There is no greater calling.

Sometimes God's agenda is simply to help us refocus our priorities. One morning I was getting ready for work when I stopped to check my calendar to see what the day had in store. I discovered that my schedule was booked with meetings that would take me well into the evening. From that moment, I decided to privately whine about what the next twelve hours would bring. On the way to work, I stopped at a local Catholic Church to attend Mass hoping that a change of surroundings might assist me in an attitude adjustment.

There is a part in the liturgy where the priest invites the congregation to offer a sign of peace to those closest to them. Reaching forward to shake the hands of the two teenagers in front of me, I was startled when they turned around, smiled, and said, "Peace be with you." Shocked at their appearance, I suddenly realized how selfish I was to complain about my "bad day." Both boys were deformed. I later learned that they were from Haiti and visiting this country so they could have plastic surgery on their disfigured faces. These two strangers, like the visitor in the chapel and the marketing student who attended my presentation, provided unexpected blessings. Hopefully, my experience will serve to challenge others to search their past for the times God sent His messengers into their life.

Choices

I have attempted to provide moral choices that most, if not all of us, will face in this world. Sharing our gifts, serving others, giving of our time, making a commitment, and demonstrating courage, humility, and compassion, round-out seven critical decisions that will ultimately determine how we will spend eternity. The choice is ours. We can create our own path or we can let society do it for us. We can do whatever it takes to be wealthy forgetting that the size of our fortune will not change our destiny. We can ignore the needs of those who love us as we journey to loneliness. We can pay homage to the calendar, iPOD, or pager, allowing "soulless" objects to control our lives. We can go back on our vows and promises, choosing conflict over harmony. We can refuse to be counted, take a stand, or set an example, letting others take the fall. We can remind family, friends, neighbors, teammates, coworkers, and a host of other individuals, how fortunate they are to walk in our presence, failing to realize that the world does not revolve around us. We can judge others according to our rules ignoring the reality that we will be judged by God's rules. We can do all these things. Or we can:

- recognize that happiness is achieved through the happiness of others.
- accept our station in life as an opportunity to fulfill our calling.
- thank God for His silence, His "NO," and His mystery.
- know that happiness is what we desire; blessedness, what God desires.
- concentrate on life's joys, instead of life's sorrows.
- put things in perspective, lest we lose touch with what's important.
- understand that happiness and selfishness will never meet.
- "smile" to ensure that the universal symbol for happiness is understood.
- live each day as if it is our last. It may be.
- invest our material blessings in this world, in preparation for the next.
- know that the beauty of our soul, not body, is what God will judge.
- use our intellect for greater good, avoiding intellectual snobbery.
- build relationships through trust and sacrifice, not deceit and narcissism.
- avoid gratifications that promise happiness, but deliver despair.
- use both privilege and power to do God's will.
- realize that both rich and poor will be in Heaven; the reverse is also true.
- serve others, placing our personal wants and needs in the proper order.
- give our time, energy, and spirit to those we love and who love us.
- be faithful to our family, employer, country, and God.
- recognize that evil, sin, and Hell exists; to ignore this truth is spiritual suicide.
- support compassion that protects life; reject that which destroys life.
- use our freedom to worship the same God who gave us this freedom.
- trade our "right" to be happy for our "right" to sow happiness.

- be proud of who we are, what we have, and what we are called to do.

- forgive others as God forgives us.

If we focus on these behaviors, then we are well on our way to eternal happiness.

Quo Vadis?

The English translation is, "Where are you going?" Are you trying to find a place where happiness is all but guaranteed? You won't find it in this world. But what you will discover is the opportunity to seek your calling. All you need to do is ask God how best you can serve Him. He will open your eyes, heart, and soul to the spiritual assignment waiting for you. For some, the journey may demand a series of encounters with those you work with and/or work for. For others, your role as neighbor, relative, teacher, or stranger may well determine what you are supposed to do with your life. In all cases, the gifts you have been given must be accounted for while suffering and sacrifice must be accepted. There will be those among you who will wander through life until God is ready to send you an invitation. Others will know at an early age what they are supposed to do with that same invitation. In all cases, you still have a choice. You can trust this world with all its illusions, or trust in the next world with all its realities. The key to your decision is to realize that you are NOT in control of the universe around you. Or as the Greek philosopher Epictetus put it, *"There is only one way to happiness and that is to cease worrying about things which are beyond the power of our will."*

There are three men I know whose spiritual journey testifies to Epictetus' wisdom. Danny grew up in a drug-invested environment. Even so, his academic and athletic prowess led him to a nationally known university where he received his higher education. While there, he met some students who suggested that he might become a Christian missionary. This calling eventually led him to the seminary where he fully intended to become a priest. One year before his ordination he received an assignment in Mexico where he met "Maria." Today, Danny and Maria have three children and the former seminarian is now teaching his students what "quo vadis" is all about.

Ray wanted to be an engineer. But his desire to help others was the impetus to change his career. He became a psychologist specializing in parenting issues. It wasn't long before his experience and personal gifts as both a writer and presenter led to the publication of three books and over two hundred presentations a year. Ray's popularity continued with television appearances, his own radio show, and production of numerous tapes and videos. Because of his love for his faith, Ray has added a new chapter in his life as a Catholic apologist, one who argues in defense or justification of church doctrine. In his free time, Ray and his wife Randi are the proud parents of ten adopted children.

Because Denny was at the top of his class in high school, he was given the opportunity to attend General Motors Institute for a future career in engineering. After only two semesters, he dropped out of school and began a journey wandering from one manual job to another. Returning to college he changed his focus and landed an accounting position with a hospital. His leadership skills set the stage for a career in hospital administration. This experience has propelled him to the top position of a 300 million dollar organization where his gifts of compassion, integrity, and stewardship, have set the bar for other healthcare leaders. As I write this copy, the song *"Amazing Grace"* is playing on the radio. The words, *"I was once blind, but now I see,"* articulate Denny's epiphany as he guides both hospital and community leadership to the highest calling possible—to serve others.

Danny, Ray, and Denny have three things in common: They changed course. They found their calling. And they serve others. For these gentlemen, "Quo Vadis" has been answered.

The Gift

Every day in every corner of the globe, there are people who are chosen to do the "little things" that make a difference in the lives of others. From the grandchild whose smile melts the heart of her grandparents, to the parents who love their Down's Syndrome child, we are reminded that there is still joy in the world. We have all had the opportunity to experience the power of kindness and its impact on the human spirit. The following scenarios represent a "servant leadership" menu from day-to-day heroes who accepted the call to serve:

- When a wife is asked who was most responsible for her physical recovery, she chooses a housekeeper over all the medical professionals because the cleaning lady taught the patient never to give up hope.

- A dying cancer patient sends flowers to the nursing staff, thanking them for their kindness and compassion.

- A bank teller wins an award for her outstanding customer service, even though her mind is preoccupied with the terminal illness of her husband.

- A grandmother brings laughter to others as she articulates the daily challenges she faces with cerebral palsy.

- A woman hands a cashier ten dollars, to cover the grocery bill of a stranger in front of her who didn't have enough food stamps to buy groceries for her family.

- To help a stranger, a maintenance man changes a tire in a raging blizzard.

- A physician drops everything she was doing, to comfort a young mother who is alone in the maternity ward crying over the possible death of her son.

- An athletic trainer shaves his head to convince a fourteen-year-old patient to have her head shaved, so an MRI can determine if the patient's injury includes internal bleeding.

- A hospital orderly drops what he is doing to help an elderly man in a wheelchair, save his dignity by taking him to the bathroom, helps change his diaper, and stays with him until his test is done.

- A social worker calls her husband on her lunch hour to go with her to a clothing store so they can buy some new clothes for a homeless man.

- A shoe shiner donates $100,000 in tips to help poor children receive free medical care.

None of these individuals were motivated by personal gain. They simply "delivered the unexpected" as they were driven by a desire to reach out to people they didn't know. Their unselfishness represents what I believe British Prime Minister Benjamin Disraeli (1874–1880) meant when he said, *"Action may not always bring happiness; but there is no happiness without action."*

On a final note, I recently had a conversation with a gentleman named Steve Winegar about the power of the human spirit. During our talk he shared a brief story about his Aunt Gerry. This lady contracted polio in the late 1930's. Aside from the hardship on her family caring for their daughter, her mom and dad had difficulty selling the milk from the family farm because no one in the community understood how polio was transmitted. Gerry almost died and eventually ended up crippled her whole life. Nevertheless, she eventually married, had four children, was active in the community, and held leadership positions in many civic organizations.

Steve told me that at her 50th wedding anniversary, she was strapped in a motorized wheelchair and only able to be out of bed for one hour per day. She needed constant care and was attended to around-the-clock by her loving husband, Stuart. Gerry had endured dozens of operations and was suffering from post-polio syndrome when she died. Before she passed away, Steve asked his favorite aunt what she would have liked to change in her life. Gerry thought for a moment, looked at her nephew, and said, "Nothing. My life's been perfect."

For Gerry, her life's calling had nothing to do with a personal pursuit of happiness; but it had everything to do with making others happy. And at the end of the day, there is no greater vocation.

EPILOGUE

Inspirations

On February 11, 1858, in the little town of Lourdes, France, located at the foot of the Pyrenees mountains, Bernadette Soubirous, a fourteen-year-old peasant girl had the first of eighteen apparitions of a beautiful Lady. As mentioned in the opening sentence of the prologue, this story was eventually told in the movie *The Song of Bernadette*.

During the apparition of March 25, 1858, Bernadette asked the Lady who turned out to be the Blessed Virgin Mary to state who she was. "*I am the Immaculate Conception*," came the reply. Mary's response confirmed a doctrine of the Catholic Church that states that the Mother of God was born without original sin. In the Church's calendar, the *Feast of the Immaculate Conception* is celebrated on December 8. This is the same day I was born.

I choose to mention this "coincidence" because as long as I can remember I have had a special devotion to the Mother of God. And throughout my life, the Blessed Virgin Mary has watched over Her servant. When I was five years old, my mother prayed incessantly to Mary asking that her polio-stricken son be healed of the dreaded disease. Because my spiritual Mother said yes, I lived a normal childhood without the stigma of braces, crutches, or a wheelchair.

When I was ten, I forgot to tell my mother that I would be late from school because I had to attend a safety-boy meeting. Rushing home I found our house empty. Instinctively, I knew that my mother would be frantic and was probably combing the neighborhood looking for her son. Realizing the seriousness of the situation, I fell on my knees and said a little prayer to Mary asking for Her help. Seconds later, the phone rang. My mother was on the other end of the line. "Son, I'm sorry I'm not home yet but my supervisor asked me to work overtime." I knew Mary said yes again. This was confirmed when my mom mentioned that it had been over three years since she had to work past four o'clock in the afternoon.

A few days before Cindy and I were to be married, I remember thinking how wonderful it would have been if my granddad were alive so he could have attended the ceremony. That night I had a very memorable dream. I saw myself standing on the altar waiting for Cindy to walk down the aisle. Instead of the organist playing the traditional rendition of "*Here Comes the Bride*," I heard the beautiful song "Ave Maria." Startled with the change of music, my attention was drawn to the back of the church where I saw my granddad standing. I left the altar, passed by my beautiful Cindy (you would think that would have been the cue that this was a dream) and walked up to the figure from my past. "Granddad, what are you doing here?" I asked. He smiled and said, "Son, I wasn't going to miss your wedding day." A few weeks later I wrote my Uncle Robert who lived in Scotland, to share the details of the wedding and the strange dream I had about his father. A short time later, a letter arrived. One sentence stood out in my uncle's correspondence. "David, 'Ave Maria' was your granddad's favorite hymn and you can bet that he was a guest at your wedding!" Again, Mary said yes!

Ten years ago I became a Knight of Immaculata, promising to say a daily rosary, pray for those who offend God, and do whatever Our Lady asks of me. A few years ago I called Marytown, the national headquarters, to make sure they still had my name on their register. Though I knew they were located in Illinois, I had no idea that the national shrine was only forty miles north of Chicago in Libertyville, Illinois. After speaking with Brother Pasqual, he inquired as to whether or not I had an interest in attending their annual retreat. Since my daughter was attending DePaul University at the time, I thought it would be a good opportunity to visit both Kelly and Marytown. "Good," Brother Pasqual said, "I only have one slot left and it's yours." The following day I went on their website to learn more about their history, facilities, and retreats. As I was scrolling down, I came across a list of books, videos, and CDs that they were selling through their gift shop. Suddenly, I came to their book-of-the-month selection where the organization was featuring "*Desiderata: A Teenager's Journey to God.*" I wrote that book based on the *Joyful, Sorrowful, and Glorious Mysteries of the Rosary*. I knew right then and there, I was meant to go to Marytown home of the Knights of Immaculata. My initial visit eventually led to ten additional trips, eight presentations, and the production of a 6-CD package honoring the Mother of God. Mary invited her servant, and he said yes!

Last October I had the honor to speak at a regional meeting of the *Blue Army*, an organization dedicated to *Our Lady of Fatima*. The regional delegate who invited me asked if I could switch my presentation time from a morning to afternoon timeslot as the presenter from the Trinitarian Sisters needed to leave right after lunch. I found out later that this religious order serves the poorest of the poor in Mexico and other parts of the world. Arriving at the church hall just before noon, I had the opportunity to listen to the order's Mother Superior. I was profoundly moved by Mother Lilly's words and humility. After her presentation the group attended Mass and then returned to the banquet hall for lunch. An hour later I was introduced to the audience and began my presentation.

During my talk, I noticed that Mother Lilly and five of her Trinitarian sisters were still in the audience. Moments after my address, a gentleman walked up to me and said, "Mother Lilly wants to speak with you." This holy woman and the other ladies in her order were waiting for me near the building's exit. As I approached Mother Lilly, she said, "David, I must give you a gift. Will you promise to wear it?" Puzzled I said, "Mother Lilly, please, you don't have to give me anything." Gently raising her hand she proceeded to remove a 3x2 inch solid bronze medal from her habit. "Promise me," she said, "that you will always wear this medal." Her gift to me was the *Medal of the Immaculate Conception,* also known as the "*Miraculous Medal.*" The inscription reads: "O Mary, conceived without sin, pray for us who have recourse to thee." The image of this medal was given to Saint Catherine Laboure, a Sisters of Charity nun, on November 27, 1830 during an apparition of the Blessed Virgin Mary.

One month after my presentation to the Blue Army, I watched *The Song of Bernadette* where Her words, "*I cannot promise you happiness in this world, only in the next,*" inspired me to write this book.

Mary's invitation continued when Bob Heintz the oldest son of Tat, the lady mentioned in the chapter on "*Choice #5: Conviction or Complacency,*" stopped by my office to share another inspiring story about his niece, Katie. This sixteen-year-old three sport star had everything going for her: Intelligence, attractiveness, popularity, athletic skills, a loving family, and both a strong character and spiritual maturity. And then it happened. Katie was diagnosed with leukemia. For many months she battled. She inspired others. But ultimately she surrendered to the Will of God.

The day before Katie passed away an aunt and uncle from Florida flew up to Michigan to say their goodbyes. This couple had two children, ages three and five, whom they left with their grandmother in the sunshine state. Katie died at one o'clock on a Sunday morning. Two hours later and fourteen hundred miles away, a three-year-old child got up from her bed, ran into Grandma's room and said, "Grandma, wake up." "What's the matter, honey?" her grandmother asked. "Grandma, we've got to call Mommy and Daddy. I just spoke to God and He told me to tell them that Katie is happy!"

Though I never met Katie, I couldn't help but sense a special affection for this girl whose faith inspired an entire community. My feelings for her were confirmed when I read an article in her hometown newspaper, the *Traverse City*

Record. Staff writer Jeff Peek talked about how many people loved and respected her. He mentioned how her life was a triumph over death. He talked about the admiration coaches, teachers, and friends had for this very special young lady. And then Mr. Peek wrote something else: "*While Katie was in the sixth grade, Cleland (principal of Katie's middle school) showed her and her classmates a movie about the Miracle at Lourdes, which told the story of St. Bernadette's vision of the Blessed Virgin Mary.*" The author went on to say that Katie was so inspired by the film that she said to the principal, "We need a place to go outside and pray." Her words inspired the building of a grotto that now stands in front of St. Francis High School in Traverse City, Michigan. Katie and Bernadette had three things in common. Both suffered. Both loved the Mother of God. And both are now enjoying eternal happiness.

An Invitation

There is a command from the Blessed Mother recorded in the Gospel of John that sets the tone for how we should try to live our life. "*Do whatever He tells you*" (Jn 2:5), is a simple directive that encompasses the seven choices discussed throughout this book. Said another way, all we need do is listen to Mary's Son. And to that end, I leave you with…a final pondering.

RUMINATIONS

In your pursuit of happiness, never lose sight of the ten simple rules that God established centuries ago. Love Him, don't use bad language, go to church, be obedient, protect the sanctity of life, have a pure heart, give an honest day's work, tell the truth, be faithful, and never succumb to jealously. These decrees are not suggestions. Abstain from truth debates. Good and evil were established long ago. Speak of values, morals, and the Ten Commandments. Let these tenets magnify your freedom of expression. Censor evil, not God. Remember, freedom of speech is a gift. Use it. Educate your soul. Verbalize your morality condemning all immorality.

Your character is built to withstand disappointment, embarrassment, and sadness. Each will surely surface. Material gifts must give way to time, for the latter creates memories. When necessary, learn to confront rather than compromise avoiding humanistic terms of endearment, entitlements, victimology, and self esteem. Too often such descriptions weave a tapestry of despair. Reject manmade treaties designed to promise happiness. They will never stand the test of time.

Never forget those that love you. Always forgive those who have forgotten you. Fidelity is not an option. But only you can decide whether your promise to love, honor, and obey is worth the effort. Be careful not to trade eternal happiness for worldly temptations.

Make peace with your neighbor. Love your spouse. Honor your father and mother. Forgive your enemies. Pray for the poor, the sick, the persecuted, those who live in war, and those who are dying a spiritual death. But for the grace of God go you. Avoid judging others lest you be judged.

Appreciate the simple things in life. A sunny day, a child's laugh, a flower's bloom, a puppy's kiss are all reasons to smile; reasons to be happy; reasons to be grateful. If you do not believe this, ask people with fourth stage cancer and they will confirm what's really important in life. Time is your gift from God. Use it wisely for you do not know the day or the hour.

Do not miss the opportunity to sow the seeds of happiness in this world because you are too busy, too engaged in your favorite football team, or caught up in the outcome of American Idol, Donald Trump's apprentice selection, or who has been chosen for the next makeover. Avoid meditations on the mystery of life, or culture of death. Neither will fulfill your calling.

Be prepared to enter your Garden of Gethsemane when you face spiritual bankruptcy; you turn from the poor, the lonely, the confused, the sick, and those in despair; when others need your personal strength and prayers to help them overcome the temptation of drugs, gambling, abortion, alcohol, pornography, greed, lust, slander, and pride; when you need to talk about all you've done and failed to do; when you fail to take care of your body and soul; or when you complain about the "cross" you are asked to carry, or fail to recognize the cross others are carrying, or worse yet, add an additional burden to those who are carrying a cross. Always be on guard when you begin to believe that the good in your life is due solely to your talents.

When these things happen pray that the spirit of God will provide you with the wisdom needed to discern right from wrong, good from evil. Forgive those whose indifference and/or ignorance can lead to distraction and/or destruction. Be passionate in your advocacy for truth, justice, and love. Stay out of the DARC, avoiding despair, alienation, radicalism, and cynicism. Trust your guardian angel to warn against impending darkness. Never trust the minions of Hell who live in eternal darkness. Focus on your spiritual journey. Be courageous as you are challenged to defend your beliefs. Build relationships with those whose compassion and commitment to the happiness of others mirrors your own. And of your own free will, use your talents for the greater glory of God.

Do all these things and you are well on your way to eternal happiness. Even so, declining morals, dark statistics, and attacks on the sanctity of life, will always be. Do not be deceived. Do not miss the time of your visitation. Do not deny Him who has the power to deny you. Do not be afraid.

For one day you will stand before almighty God and He will ask what you did with what He gave you, how you served others, what you did with your time, whether you were faithful to your obligations, what you stood for, whether you shared your blessings, and if you forgave those who trespassed against you.

How you answer then is dependent on what you do now. And what you do in this world will determine what you will do in the next. Never forget, that all you have received from God must be repaid with interest. And if you make the right choice in how you invest your time, your talent, and your treasure, you will come to realize that happiness is not reserved for this world: Only in the next.

NOTES

1. All scriptural references are directly from *The New American Bible, Saint Joseph Edition.*

2. All references to books with the word "Happiness" in the title were provided by *Borders Inc.* on August 27, 2005.

3. All "Happiness" quotes were selected after an Internet word search. Many quotations can be found in web sites promoting the history of the individual quoted (i.e. Mother Teresa, Kin Hubbard, Abraham Lincoln, et al.), or on sites like *Quoteland.com.*

4. From the chapter on *The Pursuit of Happiness,* the story on the two lottery winners was reported in the Chicago Tribune, December 29, 2004.

5. From the chapter on *Wealth or Poverty,* Michael D. O'Brien's article comes from the *Mother of All Peoples* website.

6. From the chapter on *Self or Others,* Regis Philbin's quote on Gerry Faust is direct from David Paul Eich's book, *Desiderata: A Teenager's Journey to God.* p. 165

7. From the chapter on *Pride and Proper Pride,* references on the Pope John Paul II funeral coverage were reported on the *ZENIT News Agency* website of April 16, 2005.

8. From the chapter on *Pride and Proper Pride,* Victor Frankl's quote can be found on p. 76 of his book *Man's Search For Meaning,* third edition, published by Simon and Schuster, 1984.

9. From the chapter on *Pride and Proper Pride,* Fr. William Saunders full article, *Gifts of the Holy Spirit,* may be found on the *Catholic Educator's Resource Center* website.

David Paul Eich
Keynote Presentations and Retreats

<u>Happiness, Only in the Next.</u> This keynote presentation (75 minutes), and/or retreat package (full day or weekend retreat), presents 7 choices that may determine how each of us will spend eternity.

<u>Desiderata, A Teenager's Journey to God.</u> Teens and parents experience saints and contemporary heroes through the Immaculate Heart of Mary. (*60–75 minutes*)

<u>Back To the Family.</u> Memories from 100 outstanding families demonstrate how the best of parents raise, and are raised, by their children. (*60–75 minutes*)

<u>The Gift of Change.</u> People touch our lives that we may touch the lives of others. Unsuspected blessings from the, "Visitor," "Eureka," "Bump to Bump," and the "12 Gifts," will be shared during this emotional presentation. (*60–75 minutes*)

<u>Conquering the Culture: The Fight for Our Children's Souls</u>. Exposes 5 evils. Themes include: "In Search of Morals," "If I only had a brain," "Hell's Heroes," "Rights/Responsibilities/Revolution," & "To Face the Wind." (*60–75 minutes*)

<u>First Saturday Seminar.</u> Through the mystery of the Rosary, attendees begin to fulfill Our Lady of Fatima's *First Saturday* request. (*Full day workshop*)

<u>20/20: Perfect Mystery/Perfect Vision</u>. Attendees experience profound spiritual lessons by answering the question, Quo Vadis? (60–*75 minutes*)

<u>Gethsemane: An Invitation to Eucharistic Adoration</u>. It's not a question of time or energy. It's the reality that the words, "Remember Me" represent not only what you ask of Jesus, but what the Son of God asks of you. (60–75 minutes)

For information on any of David's presentations or retreats, email: <u>DPE22@aol.com</u>

978-0-595-39273-5
0-595-39273-3

Made in the USA
Lexington, KY
09 December 2009